# Notes

## on the

# Battle of Waterloo

# NOTES

## ON THE

# BATTLE OF WATERLOO

### BY

## GENERAL SIR JAMES SHAW KENNEDY KCB

*The Spellmount Library of Military History*

SPELLMOUNT
Staplehurst

*British Library Cataloguing in Publication Data:*
A catalogue record for this book is available
from the British Library

Copyright © Spellmount Ltd 2003
Introduction © Ian Fletcher 2003

ISBN 1-86227-166-6

First published in 1865
This edition first published in the UK in 2003
in
The Spellmount Library of Military History
by
Spellmount Limited
The Old Rectory
Staplehurst
Kent TN12 0AZ

Tel: 01580 893730
Fax: 01580 893731
E-mail: enquiries@spellmount.com
Website: www.spellmount.com

1 3 5 7 9 8 6 4 2

Printed in Great Britain by
T.J. International Ltd
Padstow, Cornwall

# INTRODUCTION

Waterloo! Was there ever such a name to conjure images of stoic heroism, of the clash of arms, of bravery in the face of the 'unremitting shower of death', and of glory, not that there was anything truly glorious about the aftermath of the battle fought on 18 June 1815. On the moming after, the small, confined area along the ridge of Mont St Jean presented a spectacle that was truly a human disaster area, with thousands of dead and dying men lying strewn across the bloody fields. Waterloo! The name echoes down the ages and even today, almost two hundred years on, it continues to stir and excite a readership hungry for more words on how the first and greatest Napoleonic empire came crashing to a bloody and abrupt end on the field of battle.

Hardly a year passes without at least one more contribution to Waterloo literature. And yet, despite being one of the most documented battles in military history, Waterloo continues to defy historians and leave us groping in the dark on many aspects of what many would have us believe was a far more complex and controversial campaign that it would appear to be. Arguments continue to rage, whilst accusations of duplicity, of secrecy, and of cover-ups fly as thick as grapeshot ever did on the ridge of Mont St Jean. The truth may well be very simple; that Waterloo was a straightforward victory of the Anglo-Dutch and Prussian armies of Wellington and Blücher over the French army of Napoleon. It may well be that, ever since that momentous day, historians of the participant nations, in an effort to glean every last grain of glory from the victory, have been wasting their time trying to inflate their own contribution to victory or endeavouring to diminish their allies' share of glory. Surely there was enough glory and honour for all to be found on, 'the last great heap of glory,' that such arguments are immaterial. It is, however, unlikely that nationalistic fervour will ever be sufficiently doused, such is the nature of the Battle of Waterloo, and what may well have been simply a crushing victory of two allied armies over their enemy will never be viewed as such. Sadly, the plots and plotters are far too thick for this to happen.

The victorious armies had barely departed the great slaughter house that was the field of Waterloo than questions began to be asked of the conduct of certain officers and regiments, and of the decisions, strategies and tactics employed by the army commanders, It is these questions and the debates that continue to rage, even today, that make Waterloo one of the most controversial battles in military history. Whilst it can be argued that, from the Britain of 2003, we may read more into the battle and campaign than was actually the case in 1815, there is no doubt that certain aspects of the battle, fought on 18 June, still demand examination. With the passing of almost two hundred years, any accurate judgements on the conduct of the campaign are, of course, doomed to failure, no matter what we may like to tell ourselves.

Fortunately, we are blessed with more than our fair share of eye-witness accounts, for scores of survivors were only too keen to put pen to paper – or at least to get some more literate person to commit to paper on their behalf – and tell the story of their own part in the great battle. The overwhelming majority of these eye-witness accounts were straightforward narratives. However, one eye-witness took a different approach. In 1865, fifty years after the battle, and in the year of his own death, *Notes on the Battle of Waterloo,* by General Sir James Shaw Kennedy, was published. Kennedy's work took a different tack from most other Waterloo literature, it being not a blow-by-blow account of the battle, but a series of matter-of-fact statements and opinions on various aspects of the battle, such as the great French cavalry attacks, the defence of La Haye Sainte, mistakes made by the army commanders, and the movements of the three armies. The end result of Shaw-Kennedy's observations provides us with one of the outstanding works of Waterloo literature.

Shaw-Kennedy served on the Quartermaster-General's staff of the 3rd Division of Wellington's army at Waterloo, commanded by Lieutenant-General Sir Charles Alten. In fact, he was still plain Captain James Shaw, of the 43rd Light Infantry, at the time, and only took the name Kennedy following his marriage to Mary Kennedy in 1820. Born in 1788, Shaw came through Military College at Marlow and joined the 43rd (Monmouthshire Light Infantry) Regiment as an ensign in 1805. He served at Copenhagen two years later and the following year accompanied his regiment to Portugal at the beginning of the Peninsular War. He took part in the ill-fated Corunna campaign and between 1809 and 1810 served as ADC to Robert 'Black Bob' Craufurd, the fiery commander of the Light Division. In fact, Shaw was close to Craufurd when the latter was mortally wounded during the storming of Ciudad Rodrigo on the night of 19 January 1812. Shaw dragged Craufurd, who had been shot through the spine, away from the glare of the explosions in the breaches and out of the line of fire. He evidently returned to the fray afterwards for the regimental history of the 43rd records that it was Shaw who delivered Wellington's summons to surrender to the governor of Ciudad Rodrigo, General Barrie. Later that same year, Shaw saw action at the siege and storming of Badajoz, at the siege of the Salamanca forts and at the battle of Salamanca itself on 22 July 1812. Unfortunately, he was present during the terrible retreat from Burgos, also in 1812. This harrowing episode brought on such deterioration in Shaw's health that he was obliged to return home to England and was fated not to return for the final triumphs of 1813 and 1814.

His health had recovered sufficiently for him to return to the Colours when news of Bonaparte's escape from Elba was received in London. He was appointed Deputy-Assistant-Quartermaster-General, of Charles Alten's 3rd Division, a division composed of British, Hanoverian and King's German Legion troops. However, when Major Jessop, the Assistant-Quartermaster-General was wounded at Quatre Bras on 16 June, Shaw was left in sole charge of the Quartermaster-General's department of the 3rd Division. It was he who reconnoitred the passage of the Dyle at Bassy-Ways for his division on 17 June when Wellington retreated from Quatre Bras to the position at Mont St Jean, a vital task carried out with Bonaparte's army literally breathing down their necks.

Throughout the trial of battle on 18 June Shaw fought with his division which was positioned – largely under his own personal direction – immediately to the west of the vital crossroads which marked the centre of Wellington's position. As such, Shaw witnessed at close quarters the French cavalry attacks, the ill-fated attacks by both the Luneburgers, and by Christian Ompteda's 5th Line Battalion of the KGL. He also saw the final, dramatic attack of Bonaparte's Middle Guard during its failed assault on the Allied line towards the close of the day. Indeed, it should not be forgotten that it was not only the British Foot Guards who dealt the knockout blow against the Imperial Guard. A combination of Halkett's, Kielmansegge's and Detmar's brigades had a hand in the final repulse also. Despite being under fire on one of the hottest parts of the battlefield Shaw escaped relatively unscathed. He had one horse killed beneath him and one wounded, whilst he himself suffered a slight wound when a shot dashed the hilt of his sword to pieces before striking him in the side. With the campaign at an end, Shaw was appointed as commander at Calais during the period of the occupation of France.

It was, no doubt, during this period of relative calm, and during the post-war years, that Shaw put pen to paper and began to make his *Notes*. It is interesting that Shaw did not shy away from criticisms of his chief, in particular his handling of the forward bastion in the centre of his line, the farm of La Haye Sainte. Garrisoned initially by around 350 men of the crack 2nd Light Battalion of the King's German Legion, under the command of Major George Baring, the defenders defied everything the French threw at them until, with their ammunition virtually expended, they, or at least just 42 survivors, were forced to abandon the post and flee to the relative safety of the main Allied line. It presented Wellington with probably the greatest crisis of the battle, for the French were allowed to bring their guns to within three hundred yards of his line, from where they pounded away doing great execution. Fortunately, the loss of the farm proved not to be as critical as it might have been, for when Bonaparte launched his final attack shortly afterwards it was beaten back with heavy casualties, following which the French army's apparent march to victory turned quickly into an unstoppable rout. Shaw's close proximity to the event – coupled with the fact that he and Baring spent the night of the battle beneath Wellington's elm tree at the crossroads discussing the day's events – perhaps gave Shaw more cause than most to be critical of Wellington's apparent lack of care taken over the arrangements for the supply of ammunition to the defenders of La Haye Sainte.

Shaw's *Notes* contain several other pertinent points relating to the handling of the Anglo-Dutch army and of the course of the battle, as the reader will discover. The fog of war is notorious for obscuring what John Keegan has called, 'the personal angle of vision,' but we may take it as read that Shaw's views on the dramatic events that unfolded around him on that bloody summer's day, are as accurate, valid and as important as any other eye-witness account of the battle.

Shaw continued to serve with the army after Waterloo. After his tenure as commander of Calais during the occupation of France, he returned to England and between 1826 and 1836 served in the Adjutant-General's and Quartermaster-General's department of the army. He ended his army career as a lieutenant-general and as colonel of the 47th Regiment. His concerns with military matters continued well into his late sixties, for, upon the eve of the Crimean War, Shaw-Kennedy, as he was then called, wrote to Lord Raglan on the dangers of laying siege to Sebastopol. Having been privy to the great sieges in the Peninsula Shaw-Kennedy had seen how such operations could drain the resources of an army. We know all too well what happened in the Crimea.

Shaw-Kennedy outlived many of his contemporaries, including his old chief, and died at the age of seventy-seven on 30 May 1865, having seen not only the conclusion of the Crimean War but also the American Civil War. To me, James Shaw-Kennedy will forever be associated with Robert Craufurd and his Light Division during their tremendous operations in the Peninsula, particularly during the spring and summer of 1810 when the division successfully held an area of no less than four hundred square miles on the Agueda and Coa rivers in the face of mounting French pressure. For most historians, however, Shaw-Kennedy's legacy will be his fine and important set of *Notes* on the Waterloo campaign. Almost one hundred and forty years have passed since they were first published and their re-appearance is long overdue. Read them carefully and enjoy the recollections of one who was there and who lived through the 'crowning carnage,' that was the Battle of Waterloo.

Ian Fletcher
Rochester, 2003

# NOTES

ON THE

# BATTLE OF WATERLOO.

BY THE LATE

## GENERAL SIR JAMES SHAW KENNEDY, K.C.B.,

ACTING AT THE TIME OF THE BATTLE ON THE QUARTERMASTER-GENERAL'S STAFF
OF THE THIRD DIVISION OF THE ARMY.

WITH A BRIEF MEMOIR OF HIS LIFE AND SERVICES,
AND PLAN FOR THE DEFENCE OF CANADA.

LONDON:

JOHN MURRAY, ALBEMARLE STREET.

1865.

LONDON : PRINTED BY WILLIAM CLOWES AND SONS, STAMFORD STREET,
AND CHARING CROSS.

# CONTENTS.

# AUTOBIOGRAPHICAL MEMOIR

OF

# GENERAL SIR JAMES SHAW KENNEDY, K.C.B.

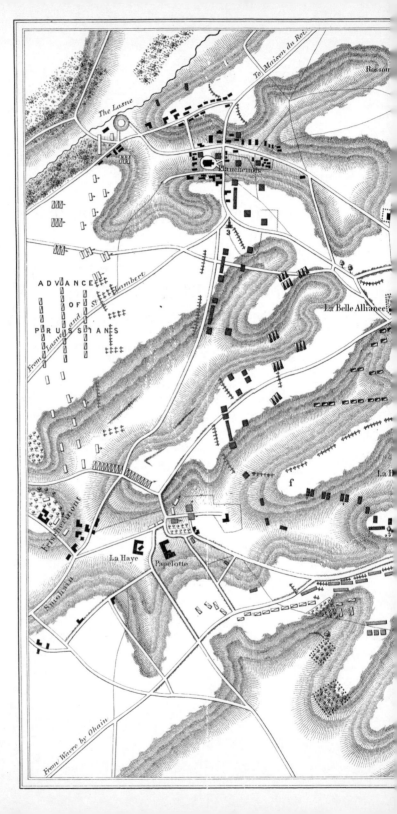

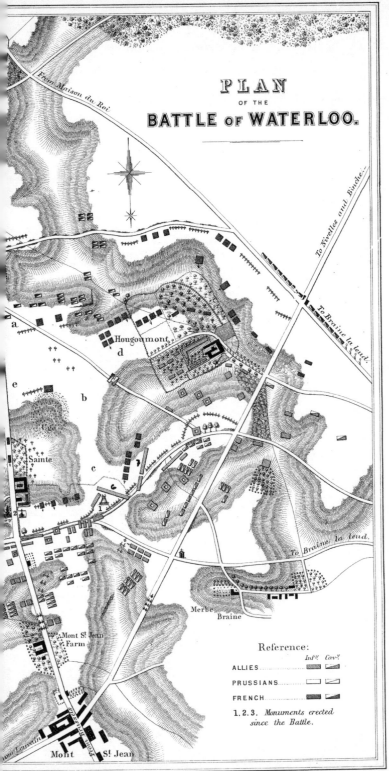

# PLAN
### OF THE
## BATTLE of WATERLOO.

From Maison du Roi

To Nivelles and Binche

To Braine la leud.

To Braine la leud.

Hougoumont

a

d

e

b

Uge

Sainte

c

Merbe
Braine

Mont St Jean
Farm

Mont St Jean

from Louvain

**Reference:**

| | Infy | Cavy |
|---|---|---|
| ALLIES | | |
| PRUSSIANS | | |
| FRENCH | | |

1.2.3. Monuments erected
since the Battle.

Kell, Bros Lith?s Castle St Holborn, London.

# AUTOBIOGRAPHICAL MEMOIR.

A MERE memoir of my services might be considered a piece of egotism; yet I feel myself so placed, since the death of the Duke of Wellington, as to wish that my friends may see a sketch or short record of those services. To solve the difficulty of giving such a sketch a general interest, I have made it a mere introduction in all its parts to the following subjects of the highest military and general interest, viz. :— First, an instance is given, to serve as example in cases of the charge of a small isolated body of infantry by a superior force of cavalry, neither party having support of any kind. Second, some isolated events of interest which took place at the sieges of Ciudad Rodrigo and Badajos. Third, the retreat from the field of battle of Quatre Bras to that of Waterloo. Fourth, the peculiar formation of the 3rd division of the army on the field of battle of Waterloo for the resistance of great attacks by cavalry (this is new, never having been given in any published account of the action), and a discussion

on grand attacks of cavalry upon infantry. Fifth,
a few authentic and important anecdotes of the Duke
of Wellington which never have been published.
Sixth, some general principles as to the management
of civil commotions.

I joined the 43rd regiment at Hythe in 1805, and
went through the course of drill and discipline put
into practice under the personal direction of Sir
John Moore. I was present at the siege of Copenhagen and battle of Kioge in 1807. I accompanied
the 43rd, in 1808, in the advance from Corunna to
Sahagoun, and during the retreat; was attacked
with violent fever after this retreat, followed by
long illness, from which I never fully recovered.
I accompanied the 43rd, in 1809, to Lisbon and to
Talavera, and there became Adjutant of the regiment.
At Campo Mayor, in 1809, I became Aide-de-camp
to Major-General Robert Craufurd; was present with
General Craufurd in the numerous affairs that took
place on the Agueda and around Ciudad Rodrigo;
and took part in that most interesting charge of
cavalry which occurred near to Villa del Puerco,
in which Colonel Talbot fell. On this occasion, from
the peculiar position on which the French infantry
formed into square, I was deputed to ride close up
to the face of the square, to ascertain its position,
before the attack was made. This cavalry attack
upon infantry will always be quoted when the much-

contested point is discussed of whether well-formed
and steady infantry can be broken by a charge of
cavalry. The French infantry, which was charged
on this occasion, consisted of,—say,—about 200 men,
commanded by Captain Gouache. The first squadron
which attacked the square consisted of a troop of
the King's German Hussars, commanded by Captain
Kraukenberge, and a troop of the 16th Light
Dragoons. Those two troops failed to break the
square, receiving a fire from its front and two faces.
I saw and heard Captain Gouache in the most distinct manner, and nothing could exceed the cool
and determined way in which he gave his orders,
and placed and kept his men in their proper places.
Captain Campbell, D.A.Q.M.G., in consequence of his
horse being shot, fell close to the bayonets of the
square ; but no man left the square, to take or touch
him, and he got up and escaped. Gouache preserved
his formation, and reserved his fire for more important objects than that of firing at, or taking, one
person. When I looked at the square before the
attack, not a shot was fired at me. The second attack
on the square was made by a squadron of the 14th
Light Dragoons, in which Colonel Talbot and the
Quartermaster were killed ; the charge was made
home into the square, but failed.

It was known to General Craufurd that detachments
of the enemy entered Barquilla and Villa del Puerco

every morning for plunder, and he determined to surprise them. For this purpose Craufurd marched at 12 o'clock at night on the 10th of July, 1810, with six squadrons of cavalry, from the neighbourhood of Fort Conception, and, leaving Alameda to the right, proceeded to a point where they dismounted and remained in the greatest possible silence, and quite concealed by a rising ground from the Gallegos road. When Craufurd saw, soon after daylight, a detachment of French infantry enter Villa del Puerco, and another of cavalry enter Barquilla, he ordered the cavalry to advance to the Gallegos road, upon which the French infantry formed into square. The cavalry found great difficulty in passing a stone enclosure that separated them from the French, and got through by slow degrees, partly at a small opening. This caused the two attacks to be made by only one squadron at each attack. Colonel Talbot and the Quartermaster; and some of the men and horses of the 14th, fell, I believe, actually on the square.

When Talbot's attack failed, Gouache moved upon Cesmiro, where the rocky nature of the ground rendered him perfectly secure against any further attack by cavalry, and there was no opportunity of charging him by the rear squadrons before he got to that situation of security, as they had been so detained and broken in their formation in passing the enclosure as not to be up and formed in time to do so.

Gouache's further retreat was, I believe, by the Quinta de Burlada to Gallegos, where the French were in force. Our loss was thirty-two killed and wounded, and nine horses, in the attack upon the French square of infantry, while, as I presume, the French square suffered no loss whatever. The thirty-one French dragoons who had entered Barquilla surrendered to our cavalry without attempting any resistance. Supports of cavalry and infantry were écheloned from Aldoa Bispo towards Barquilla in support of the cavalry at Villa del Puerco, but they took no part in the affair.

In the action which took place between Marshal Ney's corps and the Light Division, upon the investment of Almeida by the former, I received a wound in the left elbow-joint, which, owing to exfoliations of the bone, was long in healing, and prevented my serving for a considerable time.

When the siege of Ciudad Rodrigo was undertaken by the Duke of Wellington, in January, 1812, I was with General Craufurd as Aide-de-camp, and carried his Grace's summons to the governor for the surrender of the place. I accompanied General Craufurd when the Light Division advanced to storm the place, upon which occasion the General separated himself from the advancing column to about sixty yards to its left; and, placing himself on the very crest of the glacis, vociferated his orders. It must be evident to every military man, that, of all the situations he could have chosen, this was the most likely to cause his fall; he was accordingly desperately wounded; I alone was with him; no other person was at all near to us; I raised and removed him, and received from him what he considered were his dying directions. His chief direction was that I should say to his wife that "he was quite sure "that they would meet in heaven."

After General Craufurd's death I joined the 43rd, and accompanied the regiment to Badajos in 1812. I was present during the operations of the siege of the fortress, and took part in the assault. An accurate account of the attack on the breaches is given in the great work of Sir William Napier. The following is a copy of two paragraphs of that account, in which my name is mentioned :—

" In this dreadful situation, while the dead were " lying in heaps, and others continually falling, the " wounded crawling about to get some shelter from " the merciless shower above, and withal a sickening " stench from the burnt flesh of the slain, Captain " Nicholas, of the Engineers, was observed by Lieut. " Shaw, of the 43rd,[1] making incredible efforts to " force his way with a few men into the Santa Maria. " Collecting fifty soldiers, of all regiments, he joined

---

[1] "Afterwards Sir J. Shaw Kennedy."

" him, and, passing a deep cut along the foot of the
" breach, these two young officers, at the head of
" their band, rushed up the slope of the ruins; but
" ere they gained two-thirds of the ascent a concen-
" trated fire of musketry and grape dashed nearly
" the whole dead to the earth. Nicholas was mor-
" tally wounded, and the intrepid Shaw stood alone![1]
" After this no further effort was made at any point,
" and the troops remained passive, but unflinching,
" beneath the enemy's shot, which streamed without
" intermission; for many of the riflemen on the
" glacis, leaping early into the ditch, had joined in
" the assault, and the rest, raked by a cross-fire of
" grape from the distant bastions, baffled in their aim
" by the smoke and flames from the explosions, and
" too few in number, had entirely failed to quell the
" French musketry.

. . . . . . . . . .

" Let it be remembered that this frightful carnage
" took place in a space of less than a hundred yards
" square; that the slain died not all suddenly, nor
" by any one manner of death; that some perished
" by steel, some by shot, some by water; that some
" were crushed and mangled by heavy weights, some

---

[1] " Captain Nicholas, when dying, told the story of this effort,
" adding, that he saw Shaw, while thus standing alone, deliberately
" pull out his watch, and, repeating the hour aloud, declare that
" the breach could not be carried that night."

" trampled upon, some dashed to atoms by the fiery
" explosions; that for hours this destruction was
" endured without shrinking, and the town was won
" at last. These things considered, it must he ad-
" mitted that a British army bears with it an awful
" power. And false would it be to say the French
" were feeble men. The garrison stood and fought
" manfully, and with good discipline, behaving
" worthily. Shame there was none on any side.
" Yet who shall do justice to the bravery of the
" British soldiers? the noble emulation of the officers?
" Who shall measure out the glory of Ridge, of
" Macleod, of Nicholas, of O'Hare of the Rifles, who
" perished on the breach at the head of the stormers,
" and with him nearly all the volunteers for that
" desperate service? Who shall describe the spring-
" ing valour of that Portuguese grenadier who was
" killed, the foremost man at the Santa Maria? or
" the martial fury of that desperate rifleman, who,
" in his resolution to win, thrust himself beneath the
" chained sword-blades, and there suffered the enemy
" to dash his head to pieces with the ends of their
" muskets? Who can sufficiently honour the intre-
" pidity of Walker, of Shaw, of Canch, or the reso-
" lution of Fergusson of the 43rd, who, having at
" Rodrigo received two deep wounds, was here with
" his hurts still open leading the stormers of his
" regiment, the third time a volunteer, and the third

" time wounded! Nor are these selected as pre-
" eminent; many and signal were the other examples
" of unbounded devotion, some known, some that
" will never be known; for in such a tumult much
" passed unobserved, and often the observers fell
" themselves ere they could bear testimony to what
" they saw; but no age, no nation, ever sent forth
" braver troops to battle than those who stormed
" Badajos.

" When the havoc of the night was told to
" Wellington, the pride of conquest sank into a
" passionate burst of grief for the loss of his gallant
" soldiers."

Some of the circumstances stated by Sir W. Napier
I supposed were only known to myself, until I actually
read the account of them in his work; that is, circumstances which had occurred to me that I had not
mentioned, which I thought had escaped notice, partly
from the death of Captain Nicholas, and from the
fall of other officers, but which, unknown to me, had
reached Sir W. Napier. The astounding extent of
authentic information contained in his great History
will be an increasing wonder in proportion as time
affords more opportunities for testing it. In depth
of thought, eloquence, and military skill and knowledge, it is altogether unrivalled by any other military
work in our language; and that feature which will
always carry with it the highest commendation is the

uncompromising truthfulness with which it is written, although most of those who took an active share in the war were still alive when the work was published. Napier's testimony in regard to me is not merely that of an historian ; he was a Major of the regiment, and was occasionally at that time in command of the 1st battalion 43rd regiment, and knew most intimately all that occurred in it.

After the final failure, as above described by Napier, of the attack on the breach of the Santa Maria bastion, I proceeded with a very few men to the ruined ravelin in the ditch between the Trinidad and Santa Maria bastions. It afforded some slight degree of shelter from the fire of the place. Johnston of the Rifles—who was severely wounded— another officer of the Rifles, and two officers of other regiments, and a small number of men, were collected there ; and we determined to hold it till daylight, as it seemed possible, from two considerations, that it might be of great importance to do so. Lord Wellington might have wished to renew the assault at daylight, or to have established a lodgment on the crest of the glacis ; either of which our holding the ravelin would have greatly favoured. We had remained but a short time on the ravelin when a general shout was raised that the French were effecting a sortie into the ditch, which of course caused much alarm to the wounded men, and every man who could move now rushed to the ladders and got out of the ditch. There was difficulty in getting Johnston up the ladder, and he was assisted by the right-hand man of my company, whose name, I think, was Norton. This gallant soldier had done his duty admirably; a ball passed through his head, and he fell dead from the ladder.

It would be equally unfeeling, as it would be unjust, to enter into any account of the attack on the breaches without noticing the devoted and admirable conduct of the non-commissioned officers and soldiers. The noble soldier Norton did his duty in an heroic manner during the whole continuance of the attack, but I only mention him as one instance; the way in which the men stuck to and obeyed their officers was admirable; and the immense number of killed and wounded testify to the desperate nature of the service which they so faithfully performed.

Upon returning to the ditch at daylight in the morning, I found my friend Lieutenant Henry Oglander. He lay there with five wounds in his body, and by a sixth wound one of his arms was so shattered as to make immediate amputation necessary. I mention him particularly because he was a superior man, and was distinguished for coolness in the greatest dangers. He had a curious escape in going up to the attack. Being Lieutenant of the company before mine, while we were in column of sections, he was walking with me when a large shot from the Pardeleras knocked down the whole of his section—they went down like a row of nine-pins, the shot having gone through from left to right of the section.

The names of the two centurions, T. Pulfio and L. Varenus, have been immortalised by Cæsar's having had the good taste and good feeling to mention their exploit; the names of those two men will be known as long as history is read. Yet it appears from Cæsar's description, that the voluntary peril to which Pulfio and Varenus exposed themselves was vastly less than that volunteered for and executed by Captain Nicholas in his first attack on the breach of Santa Maria. It is quite possible to suppose, from Cæsar's description, that both Pulfio and Varenus should escape; but it is impossible to understand how Nicholas escaped from his first attack upon the chevaux-de-frise of the breach of the Santa Maria. He seemed determined to tear the sword-blade chevaux-de-frise from their fastenings, in which attempt he long persevered while enveloped in an absolute stream of fire and balls poured out against him by the defenders. Wellington did not know of the devoted acts of heroism of Nicholas; in this respect Nicholas was less fortunate than Pulfio and Varenus. Cæsar was unable to decide upon the comparative merit of Pulfio and Varenus;

Nicholas was unquestionably the hero of the Santa Maria.

An order was issued two or three days before the assault of Badajos, that the Light Division was to form for the assault in column on the left of the Rivellas, with the head of the column near to the quarry, and pointing to the bastion of Trinidad. This formation was to be made after dark, in the greatest silence, and the head of the column was not to pass the point at which it would become directly exposed to the shot from the place and from the fort of Pardeleras : to fix upon this point was of great importance, but difficult, because during darkness it was impossible, and during daylight success in the attempt could scarcely be expected. It was determined, however, that I should make the attempt, while Colonel M'Leod and Lieutenant Oglander posted themselves on the height of St. Michael to signalize to me as to the movements which the French might make from the place or from the Pardeleras. Commencing at a well-ascertained point on the left of the Rivellas —which point could not be mistaken even in the night—I took regular paces—counting my paces— and proceeded directly towards the bastion of Trinidad, until I got very near to the covered-way of that bastion, and saw that no further advance could be made by a column without exposure to the fire both of the bastion and of the Pardeleras.

M'Leod now made the signal indicating that the
French had sent out a party from the Pardeleras to
intercept my return. By returning at the same
measured and slow pace at which I had advanced
I accomplished two things, viz., measuring again the
distance, and imposing on the French detachment;
for they evidently were intimidated, from supposing
that I was supported. This successful measurement
of the required distance for the column to stand upon
in safety was of much importance on the night of
the assault. By it the column of the Light Division
was placed in the position from which it proceeded to
the assault.

I continued with the 43rd during the advance to
Salamanca in 1812; the taking of the forts there;
the operations on to the Douro; the retreat to Salamanca; the battle of Salamanca; the advance to
Madrid and reduction of the Retiro; and until after
the retreat from Madrid had commenced. During
the retreat I became Aide-de-camp to General Baron
Alten, commanding the Light Division, and was
with him as Aide-de-camp in the retreat to Salamanca,
and from that to Rodrigo, and in the affairs that took
place on that retreat.

After the retreat of the army from Burgos and
Madrid to Portugal and the frontier of Spain, at the
close of 1812, my health became such as to oblige me
to return to England upon medical certificates; and

this was followed by a fever of the most violent character, and of long continuance. From the effects of this fever, and some partial relapses which I had of it, I have never wholly recovered. My state of health ever since has been extremely delicate and precarious, and such as to render me unfit for severe field operations.

Having recovered, to a certain extent, from those repeated attacks of fever, I was able in 1815, upon Bonaparte's return to France from Elba, to join General Baron Alten's division—that is, the 3rd division of the Anglo-Allied army—in Belgium. Major Jessop was Assistant-Quartermaster-General of the division, and I was the Deputy-Assistant. We had not been a quarter of an hour on the field of the battle of Quatre Bras when Major Jessop was wounded, so that the whole charge of the Quartermaster-General's department for the 3rd division of the army during the 16th, 17th, and 18th of June, 1815, devolved upon me. The division was severely engaged on the 16th, and was in a position of great delicacy to be withdrawn from on the 17th, as it occupied Piermont and part of the great road towards Brye, and consequently became exposed to the advance of the army under Bonaparte from the field of Ligny. I was ordered to reconnoitre the country from the position of the division, near Piermont, to the Dyle, and to fix upon its line of retreat, and upon the point at which it should pass the Dyle, so as to leave the passage at Genappe free for the other portions of the army. The division retired upon the line as fixed upon in this reconnaissance. Marching by Bezy, it passed the Dyle by the bridge of Wais-le-Hutte, and, by a cross march, joined the great road leading from Genappe to Waterloo. This operation was a very delicate one,—that of withdrawing six thousand men from before so great a force, in open day, under Napoleon, with which force they were in actual contact, and having during their retreat to cross a considerable river. The operation was, however, perfectly successful. Every possible precaution was taken to withdraw a great portion of the division before the enemy perceived that it was moving in retreat, and the three brigades were so arranged that they kept in échelons on the line of retreat, each brigade forming on ground favourable for repelling an attack, and so that each brigade should retire in succession; thus the enemy constantly found, as he advanced, brigade after brigade regularly formed for action. Although the enemy closely followed the division, he never attempted any regular attack upon it. After having joined the great Genappe road, the division proceeded directly along that road to the field of the battle of Waterloo.

The circumstances under which the 3rd division was placed in position at Waterloo under my direc-

tions are fully described in the following account of
the battle. The unsuccessful and disastrous attacks
of the French cavalry on the division so posted I
presume to consider as the most formidable which
have been made by cavalry upon infantry since the
use of fire-arms, with the exception of that at Eylau :
that is, I consider that no other instance can be
pointed out in modern history of infantry being
attacked by an equally formidable force of cavalry,
when the numbers, composition of the force, and the
characters of the leaders of that force are taken into
consideration, and the small number of the resisting
force. The instances which seem to come nearest to
it are those of Auerstadt and Gross-Aspern. At
Auerstadt the cavalry attacks were led by Blucher
and Prince William of Prussia, in presence of the
King of Prussia. Gudin and Morand, having formed
squares in exchequer, resisted successfully. The case
of Gross-Aspern, in 1809, is still more similar to that
which took place at Waterloo. The formation of the
squares in exchequer at Gross-Aspern is said to have
been made by the Archduke Charles, in consequence
of the impression that had been made upon his mind
by the perusal of a work by Jomini, in which such a
formation was recommended ; but no such formation
was then known to the British army or in England.
The number of squadrons that charged at Gross-
Aspern was very great, probably about sixty ; the

composition admirable; and they were led by Bessières, Espagne, and Lasalle.

The cavalry charge at Eylau was led by Murat, Hautpoult, Grouchy, and Lepic, and was composed of the whole reserved cavalry and the Gardes à Cheval, amounting to, say, eighty squadrons. This charge was partly successful, and had a very beneficial influence on the result of the action in favour of Napoleon. It therefore contrasts favourably for the formation adopted by the infantry at Waterloo. The Russian infantry behaved with great gallantry; and it is fair to presume, that, with a better formation, they would have resisted successfully from the first; they did in the end, when strongly reinforced, repulse the cavalry attack. The cavalry attack at Eylau seems to me to be the only one that appears in the history of modern European wars as being made upon infantry with a greater force of cavalry than that by which the infantry was attacked at Waterloo; and in no case were the leaders more eminent, or the composition and confidence of the troops better. But here the comparison ends, for the number of the Russian infantry against whom the attack was directed was vastly greater than that against which it was made at Waterloo; and the supporting force of cavalry was also vastly greater at Eylau than at Waterloo.

Marlborough's charge upon the centre of the French position at Blenheim may be considered as having been made against much the same part of the line of battle as that made by the French cavalry at Waterloo, and up a similar slope, and made with a great body of cavalry; but the cases are totally dissimilar in principle, for Marlborough's was an attack upon cavalry; so completely so, that he even placed some infantry to face the few battalions of French infantry that were on that part of the position.

At the battle of Borodino, the bastioned field-work, and the most important central point of the field of battle, were taken by a charge of the 2nd French corps of cavalry; but there again the comparison fails entirely, for the attacking force consisted of both cavalry and infantry, and the attack was not made until the Russian line had suffered enormous loss by repeated attacks of infantry, and by cannonade. The cavalry charge at Eckmuhl was perhaps the most formidable of modern times of cavalry against cavalry, but it was purely a cavalry affair. Hannibal's victories were won chiefly by charges of cavalry upon infantry,[1] in which the numbers may have been as great as those in the French charges at Waterloo; but the instances of cavalry charges upon infantry prior to infantry's being armed with the musket, and protected by the fire of artillery, are valueless as

---

[1] See 'Mémoires de Napoléon, par Montholon,' vol. ii. pp. 137, 138.

comparisons with charges of cavalry upon infantry so armed and so protected.

It will occur to every one, on perusing the above narrative as to the formation of the 3rd division in order of battle, that the formation was in fact made in a manner that was contrary to that which was ordered by the Duke of Wellington, as implied in his short direction, "Form in the usual way." In explanation of this seeming departure from the literal words of the order, it is to be observed that the formation was made under the observation of his Grace, and that his allowing it to remain unchanged stamped it with his sanction.

The formation of battalions on the two central companies, and their being placed in two lines, and so placed that when formed in oblongs they stand in exchequer,—as the 3rd division has been shown to have done at Waterloo,—seems to be the best order of battle that can be adopted, either for receiving an enemy's attack in a general action, or for approaching a position that is to be attacked. If an army is in line on a position, and the oblong formation has been predetermined to be made in the event of an attack by cavalry, we have seen how readily and effectually that formation can be accomplished; and supposing, on the contrary, that it is required to advance for the purpose of making an attack, the oblong formation being adopted will enable a line of

any magnitude to advance in order of battle for any
required distance in the most perfect order, until so
near the enemy's artillery that deployment becomes
necessary, which, from the formation on the two
centre companies, would be more rapidly made than
from any other.   In the formation of oblongs by the
3rd division at Waterloo, to resist cavalry, the oblongs
had not the advantage of having artillery on their
flanks.   When guns are placed on their flanks, so as
to protect their fronts by a fire of round-shot or shrap-
nells first, and next of grape-shot, there cannot be any
fear for a line of battle of steady infantry if attacked
by cavalry while in this formation.   The oblongs may
be formed by battalions having any number of companies,—ten, eight, six, or four; but in each case the
flank faces must consist of only one company, formed
four deep; that is, the two subdivisions of the company are formed the one behind the other.

An anecdote of the Duke of Wellington was related
to me at Homburg by Sir Frederick Adam, which I
look upon as of much historical interest as regards the
battle of Waterloo.   When Wellington stood near
to the Nivelles road, to the right rear of Maitland's
brigade, he was near to Adam's brigade; and some
time before that brigade was moved across the road,
the Duke said to Adam, in a very brisk and animated
manner, " By G—, Adam, I think we shall beat them
" yet!"   From what other source do we know what

the Duke's feelings were, up to that period, as to the probable issue of the action ?

Two days after the battle, that is, on the 20th June, 1815, I had a long and most interesting discussion with the Duke of Wellington (in a French farmhouse) respecting the very critical moment of the battle of Waterloo when I drew his attention to the fact that that part of his line of battle immediately behind La Haye Sainte was denuded of troops.   His Grace entered minutely and closely into the detail of the occurrences, expressing his opinion and asking many questions.   This discussion arose from General Alten's report as to this part of the action having been written without his having seen what he described, as he had been obliged previously to leave the field from a wound, and his report consequently required further explanation.   Some of his Grace's questions were of a very confidential nature, and some in direct terms, as to the future arrangements of the division.   One of his Grace's questions was to this effect :—" When the gap took place in the line " of battle behind La Haye Sainte, why was not " I immediately informed ?"   To this question I answered to the following effect, if not in the precise words :—" The moment that the opening occurred I " galloped straight to your Grace, and informed you " of the circumstance when you were standing close " to the Nivelles road, and you answered by saying

" that you would order the Brunswick troops to the
" point, and more troops ; and you ordered me to
" get to the spot as many of the German troops as I
" could, and as much artillery as I could." This answer
completely satisfied the Duke ; he perfectly recollected
the circumstance, and said that he saw that all was
right, and that there was a mistake in Alten's report,
arising from his having previously left the field.

The following appears in General Alten's report of
the battle of Waterloo to the Duke of Wellington,
dated Brussels, 19th June, 1815 :—

" The services of Captain Shaw, Deputy Assistant-
" Quartermaster-General, who was senior of the de-
" partment in the absence of Major Jessop, from a
" wound, were indispensable to me for executing the
" disposition of the troops for the attack."

The following occurs in General Alten's letter to
the Duke of Wellington, dated Brussels, June 20th,
1815, recommending officers who served with the
3rd division at Quatre Bras and Waterloo :—

" Captain Shaw, Deputy Assistant-Quartermaster-
" General, whose services previous to and during the
" action were most important to me, is an officer
" who should be brought forward and placed in
" situations where his military talents can be best
" employed."

The following is the copy of a letter from General
Baron Alten to General Sir George Murray :—

"Brussels, 11th December, 1815.

"DEAR SIR,

"As I perceive by the General Orders of the 3rd
"instant, that Major Shaw, of the 43rd regiment, Assistant
"Quartermaster-General to the 3rd division, will be discon-
"tinued on the Staff from the 25th instant, I beg leave
"to inform you that his Grace the Duke of Wellington was
"good enough to appoint that officer on the Staff in May
"last, and to the 3rd division, then under my command, in
"consequence of my recommendation, which I grounded on
"a long acquaintance I had with Major Shaw in the Penin-
"sula, where he served on my Staff, and gave me an oppor-
"tunity to know his value as a Staff officer.  Since his late
"appointment in this country, and particularly during the
"actions of the 16th and 18th of June last, where he was in
"charge of the department with the division, he has again
"so much confirmed the high opinion I always entertained of
"his gallantry, zeal, and abilities, that I feel it due to him to
"bring it to your knowledge, and to say, that, should you at
"any period have an opening in the Quartermaster-General's
"department, and are disposed to fix your choice on him,
"I can with every confidence recommend him as an acqui-
"sition.

"Allow me, my dear Sir, to take this opportunity of
"assuring you how much I rejoice, together with the whole
"army, at your late appointment as Chief of the Staff to
"the Allied Army of Occupation, and how happy I should
"feel, when my health will again permit me, to enter upon
"our former friendly intercourse, both official and private.

"I remain, my dear Sir,

"Yours very faithfully,

(Signed)        "CHARLES ALTEN."

In the action (18th June) I had one horse killed and one wounded; and I was disabled for a short time by a shot which, first breaking to pieces the strong steel handle of my sword, struck me on the side.

When the army broke up from Paris, in the end of 1815, partly to form the Army of Occupation, and partly to return to England, it fell to me, as one of the junior Assistant-Quartermasters-General, to be reduced from that staff. By an oversight in the treaty by which an army was to occupy for a time certain portions of the north of France, it was omitted to be stipulated that Calais should be open to the British army as the port of communication between the British Army of Occupation and England. To correct this error, the Duke of Wellington obtained the consent of the French Government that Colonel Espinasse on the part of the French Government, and I on the part of his Grace, should meet at Calais and arrange a treaty for the partial occupation of the place by a British establishment during the time that the Army of Occupation should remain in France. This treaty was accomplished, and I was retained as Assistant-Quartermaster-General, and placed in charge of the establishment at Calais, during the whole period that the Army of Occupation remained in France.

Several embarrassing difficulties arose during this partial occupancy of Calais; these were, however,

got over, and his Grace was good enough to say, on
one of these occasions, that, but for the decisions
which I had come to when there was no possibility
of referring for instructions, he would have been
obliged to change the establishment from Calais to
Ostend.  The arrangements for the embarkation of
the Army of Occupation, and previously of a corps
of five thousand Russian troops, fell upon Captain
Hill of the navy and myself; and I received from
the Emperor Alexander an expression of thanks and
a diamond ring, through Count Woronzow, for the
embarkation of the Russian corps.

I was promoted to the brevet rank of Major, upon
the recommendation of General Alten, for the battles
of Quatre Bras and Waterloo; and upon the recommendation of the Duke of Wellington I obtained the
brevet rank of Lieut.-Colonel, after the breaking up
of the Army of Occupation.

In one of the numerous visits which the Duke of
Wellington necessarily paid to Calais, on his way
from France to England, during the continuance of
the Army of Occupation in France, when walking
from the Hôtel Dessin to the pier to embark, he said
to me that he had always made it a rule to study by
himself for some hours every day ; and alluded to his
having commenced acting upon this rule before he
went to India, and of his having continued to act upon
it.  This is a fact that I apprehend is unknown as to

the Duke of Wellington; and it is a very important one. It proves that, like Cæsar and Napoleon, and probably all the greatest men of the world, he was fully aware of the necessity of systematic and careful study. It is evident that Napoleon, before he was twenty-six, had read the works of all the great masters of war ; had analysed their campaigns, operations, and ideas; had rejected the dross, and arranged fully in his mind the good and great principles which they established ; and had thus filled his mind with such a body of principles, and such a fund of knowledge, that no state of circumstances could be presented to him that he had not the means of solving. The rapidity and correctness of his solutions, under the most complicated circumstances, seemed mysterious to those who witnessed them; but that rapidity and correctness of solution unquestionably proceeded from the fund of principles established in his mind, aided by wonderful natural powers.

In 1826 I was appointed Assistant Adjutant-General of the northern district of Ireland; and in December of the same year I was ordered to proceed to Manchester, and remained at Manchester as Assistant Adjutant-General till 1836 ; thus completing a service of ten years as Assistant Adjutant-General. I was on the staff of the Quartermaster-General's department for three years in the Netherlands and France, and thus completed altogether a service on the staff, in the situations of Assistant Quartermaster-General and Assistant Adjutant-General, of thirteen years.

It is an historical fact known to every one that the period from 1827 till 1836 was one during which very great political excitement existed occasionally in Manchester and the country around it; and also that very serious strikes and outbreaks of the work-people took place during that period in Manchester, Stockport, the Potteries, Wigan, Preston, Rochdale, Oldham, Bolton, Blackburn, Burnley, and Ashton-under-Line. The arrangements for meeting those outbreaks fell entirely upon me, as the General Officers who commanded the northern district always had their head-quarters in Yorkshire, and only went into Lancashire if specially called upon to do so under some pressing emergency.

I leave others to judge what degree of difficulty and delicacy there is in the management of so wide a district, with so great a population, when it is much disturbed. The prompt supply of troops, as they may be probably wanted; their proper distribution; the preparation of temporary barracks; the arrangements to be arrived at with the magistrates in their respective districts; and, above all, the personal command of the troops when opposing riots, are presumed here to present no trifling difficulties, if they are so managed as to prevent loss of property, and maintain the supremacy of the law and the complete authority of the magistrates, and yet so as to avoid the necessity of absolute collision and bloodshed. These objects, I presume to state, were thoroughly accomplished during the whole period of my being on the staff in the northern district, not only for Manchester, but for the whole of the surrounding district; —for the whole of Lancashire and the district of the Potteries. On leaving the district I was officially thanked in the most gratifying manner, both by the military authorities, and by the authorities at the Home Office ; and I was presented with a service of plate, accompanied by a handsome address, by the town of Manchester. The Duke of Wellington was himself at Manchester at a time of great excitement, and had a full opportunity of judging what degree of importance should be attached to the management of such a population when roused to great excitement ; a state of things now happily unknown in this country.

Having had so much experience in the actual surveillance of civil commotions in the manufacturing districts of England, and in Ireland—and the subject having been for many years under my earnest and anxious consideration—it seems proper that I should state here the heads of the principles that were acted upon in cases of civil commotion, where I either had the power in my own hands, or possessed sufficient influence to cause their being acted upon.

First.—When a military force is employed in aid of the civil power, it should be of overwhelming amount; and should, in all cases, consist of both cavalry and infantry; and whenever the commotion is of a serious character all the three arms should be employed,—cavalry, artillery, and infantry.

Second.—It will be found much more difficult than can be supposed to employ an overwhelmingly large force, even when such force can easily be collected; for it will be attributed to timidity, an accusation which military men do not like. Besides which, it always seems to the troops uncalled for, and often becomes very irksome, from the frequency of their being called out. But in the face of all difficulties it must be constantly borne in mind that using an overwhelming force for suppression of riots, and in support of the civil power, is the golden rule for accomplishing those objects without bloodshed; a consummation so highly desirable as to render every effort for its accomplishment imperative. Another advantage of the employment of a large force is that of rendering success certain, should actual collision take place. In some cases the troops should not be shown, but kept in hand, and ready to act; but in other cases, to show a large force may have a very excellent effect in a town or neighbourhood where a disposition exists to resist and overthrow the authority of the law and the civil power. From the Duke of

Wellington's having in some cases kept the troops out of public view, it seemed to be laid down as an invariable rule that this should always be acted upon. It is dangerous for men who do not study principles to lay down rules formed on a few acts of any great master. I hold that the Duke would not have acted on this as an invariable rule; if he had, I know that he would have rebuked in cases where he approved.

Third.—The most delicate and the most difficult of all decisions to be come to in civil commotions is that of judging when to take an active part—that is, an offensive part—against illegal assemblages, or when to remain only in presence of, and in readiness to meet, such assemblages. There is the greatest possible difference between those two courses; and it is often extremely difficult to determine which should be adopted. When the offensive course is adopted, the authorities adopting it—both magistrates and military —take a great responsibility upon themselves: upon them there falls the necessity of proving that their acting offensively against the people was absolutely necessary; and to do so is often extremely difficult, even where there has been an absolute necessity for acting offensively. But in addition to this consideration, it is often extremely injudicious and improper to use force to prevent assemblages, or to disperse them, in place of watching their proceedings, cautioning their leaders, and being prepared and perfectly ready with an ample force to act vigorously, should the assemblage result in the committal of such breach of the law as to render that necessary. The next most important rule to that of having a large force— as already stated—is that of putting it, when possible, in a defensive and threatening attitude, rather than that of bringing it offensively into actual collision with the people. But this has its limits; and whenever a military force is used, it should be used with determination, and made perfectly effectual. Should the magistrates come to the important determination of preventing an intended assemblage, a proclamation by the magistrates of their determination to prevent the assemblage should be widely circulated in the district: placards giving notice of it should be placed conspicuously on the ground where the assemblage is expected; and men carrying such placards on poles should be sent along the roads and approaches to the ground fixed for the assembly. The magistrates should take every means to make their determination known; and this determination, once come to and made public, should be acted upon firmly, and put into full execution, irrespective of all other considerations: the determination may be a grave one, and requires full consideration before being arrived at. When time allows, the opinion of the Government should be taken.

Fourth.—The cases in which riotous assemblages proceed to the length of injuring persons or property presents no real difficulty as to the decision of how they are to be dealt with. The magistrates will then, of course, order the seizure or dispersion of the rioters; and the military officer in command, if so called upon, will proceed to carry the decision of the magistrates determinedly into effect. This will be best accomplished, and with the least chance of casualties, by the judicious joint employment of cavalry, infantry, and police.

Fifth.—When very serious popular tumults are apprehended in large towns, a plan should be drawn out by the officer commanding the troops, and submitted for approval to the magistrates, for securing the possession of the town. To accomplish this, it is necessary to fix upon some large building, with sufficient open space adjoining to it, which is to be firmly held by the military and constables, and from which, by a line of streets fixed upon, a free communication with the country should be quite secured. The central building, and buildings in the line for keeping open the communication from the country, should be prepared for defence, and be held, when necessary, by a force of special constables, chiefly; while the military force is held in constant readiness to march to any part of the town, to make such attacks as may be found necessary. In making those attacks care must be taken not too much to divide the troops, but on the contrary to send an overwhelming force, if possible, to each point attacked. It is here assumed as an invariable rule, that in this country, in all cases of civil commotion, a comparatively large body of special constables will be sworn in and organised.

Sixth.—An unexpected difficulty occurred in cases of turnouts of the workpeople in the manufacturing districts. This arose from the turnouts adopting a system called piqueting; that is, they placed regularly-relieved sentinels upon the mills where they had struck work, so that nothing could go out or into them but under the supervision of those sentinels; and they placed sentinels in like manner on the houses of the millowners, and on their persons; for they kept them in view when they went out. This system amounted, in fact, to one of intimidation, but was so managed by the workpeople that the magistrates declared that there was no law by which those carrying it into practice could be convicted and punished. The case became so important that the highest legal authorities were consulted on the subject; and they not only confirmed the opinions of the local magistrates, but said that the case was of such extreme delicacy and difficulty that they could not recommend any attempt to inter-fere with the law on the subject as it then stood. There is, however, a practical solution; for if it is legal to place a sentinel over any tradesman, or over any one in his employment, so also it must be legal to place a sentinel over that sentinel; and if such is done, it neutralises the cruel and intimidating effect of sentinels being placed over a man's person and property. Indeed, this system led to attacks upon the masters; but if each piqueting sentry had a police-man placed as a sentinel over him, the intimidation would be balanced, and the bad effect almost done away with. But although this would be a legitimate interference to protect the masters from the effects of a very unfair and menacing system, the greatest pos-sible care should be taken not to interfere so as to show any—not even the slightest—bias or favour for either the workpeople or the masters.

In the period of about nine years, during which I was Assistant Adjutant-General at Manchester, there were three different General Officers in command of the northern district, and from each I received flatter-ing testimonials of confidence.

During this period there were several changes of administration, and consequently of Secretaries of State for the Home Department. I was authorised to, and often did, communicate with the Home Office, and sometimes did so personally. I also communicated directly on all important occasions with the Com-mander-in-Chief's office, and I certainly received from all those departments assurances of continued confi-dence; and from this, I presume to suppose, arose the proposals made to me under two Governments of different views—that I should accept situations, each of which was looked upon as of considerable national importance.

When the Metropolitan police force was about to be formed, the Secretary of State for the Home Department, Sir Robert Peel, proposed that I should be the First Commissioner; but I declined the appointment, having a reluctance to leave my own profession.

When the consolidation took place of the Irish constabulary force, I was asked, by desire of the Government, to take the situation of Inspector-General of the force, which offer I accepted, although with reluctance. The feeling which caused my refusing the first of those situations, and accepting the second, was, that the constabulary force was of a more extensive command, and was more of a military character than the other. I remained for two years Inspector-General of the constabulary force of Ireland. In that time the complete organisation of the force, amounting to 8000 men, was effected. A code of general instructions for the force was composed and carried fully into effect; also an instruction for the duties of constables; the finance arrangements for the force were fully established; and I wrote out, expressly for the use of the constabulary force, a system of drill and field exercise; and so completely was this system carried out, that any part of the constabulary force was quite in a fit state to form the advance or rear-guard of any troops with whom it might have had to act, or to have formed in a solid order of battle. It has, I think, been admitted on all hands, that the force was admirable, and that the organisation was not defective. I resigned the command of the constabulary force, but not until after the organisation was completed. Although requested to continue that command, I declined doing so.

At the time that the great Chartist demonstration took place in London—10th April, 1848—anxiety existed as to the state of Liverpool, and it had been decided upon that a body of troops and a general officer should be sent there. I had become a major-general in 1846, and was at Hastings on account of the state of my health in April, 1848. A Queen's messenger was sent to me to Hastings on the night of the 9th of April, with an order that I should assume the command of the troops at Liverpool on the 10th, which I did, and remained at Liverpool in the command of Sir William Warr's district until he recovered from an illness which had prevented his acting.

When the insurrectionary movement took place in Ireland in 1848, two additional general officers were appointed to assist in its suppression : Viscount Hardinge was one, and I was the other. I was then in Scotland, in so bad a state of health that I could not be on horseback even for an hour, and I was with the utmost reluctance obliged to renounce this most interesting appointment.

The next appointment to which I was nominated was that of Governor and Commander of the Forces of the Mauritius, and I was directed to see Earl Grey early in 1849, and proceed as soon as possible to the colony.  Of this appointment I had not the slightest previous intimation, and never had in any shape or way applied for it; but I considered it one of the best in the gift of the Crown, and very important. My anxiety to assume its functions was correspondingly great, but the bad state of my health was such that it became impossible for me even to proceed from Scotland to London to see Earl Grey on the subject, and I was thus obliged, most reluctantly, to renounce the appointment.  In Earl Grey's communication to me announcing my having been appointed Governor of the Mauritius, and Commander of the Forces, he stated that he was aware of my capabilities for the civil duties of the situation from my conduct in Manchester and Ireland; and that, upon the Duke of Wellington having been applied to, his Grace had stated that I was qualified for the military duties of the command.

In the spring of 1852 I was appointed to the command of the forces in North Britain, and the state of my health for a time gave me the hope that

I might undertake the duties of that important command. I accepted the command, and prepared to proceed to Edinburgh, but I afterwards fell into such an extremely bad state of health as to be obliged to renounce the command, and to be removed to the south of England.

I must be permitted to say that the various high and important situations and commands in which the Duke of Wellington placed me, or recommended that I should fill, arose entirely from himself. I never, on any occasion whatever, applied to his Grace for appointment, for good service pensions, or for commands; and I was made aware that those recommendations and appointments proceeded from himself. I conceive, therefore, that I am logically, and in all fairness, entitled to come to the unquestionable conclusion that the Duke of Wellington acted towards me with the consideration, which he uniformly did, from his own knowledge of my services in the field, and otherwise, as shown in the narrative : part of which were—the retreat of the 3rd division from Quatre Bras; the formation of the 3rd division in order of battle at Waterloo; my having pointed out to him the gap in the line of battle behind La Haye Sainte (the most dangerous moment of the battle), and the execution of his orders in assisting to fill it up; having conducted the communications at Calais for three years during the Army of Occupation, and made the arrangements for embarking the army and stores and a Russian corps there; having conducted for about nine years the affairs, in very troubled times, of the enormously populous district round Manchester, with its vast property, without any loss of life or property; and the organisation of the constabulary force of Ireland. The Duke of Wellington was perfectly aware of the views which I had as to civil commotions from my correspondence from Manchester, and from his having been there; and he saw plans which I drew out for the defence of Manchester, Birmingham, and Liverpool. I must add that, to my knowledge, the Duke of Wellington had himself carefully considered the subject of civil commotions.

Since the above was written I have read the first two volumes of the Life of that highly distinguished officer, Sir Charles James Napier, by his brother, Sir William Napier. Sir Charles Napier was not only highly distinguished as an officer, and commander of armies in the field, but also for great originality and depth of thought. To these great qualities he added the charm of unbounded candour and ingenuousness. His Life, therefore, coming from the classic pen of Sir William, will undoubtedly be a standard work. It gives me unfeigned pleasure to find that Sir Charles has noticed my friend

General Wemyss and myself in reference to the disturbed state of the northern district. Wemyss, whose gallant services with the chivalric and able Barnes, and on many hard-fought fields besides, are well known, has now a testimonial from a perfectly pure source—that of a great man who knew him well and intimately.

The following is the copy of a paragraph in the 'Life of Sir Charles Napier' in which I am mentioned :—

" 25th. All quiet. Read a report made by Colonel " Shaw Kennedy to the police commissioners on the " subject of rioters. He was long at Manchester, " and this report is a most masterly affair; I have " felt more at home since reading it, but my task is " harder than his, for a greater power is against me. " He had only to deal with workmen fighting against " their masters; I have to deal with a large mass of " the population avowedly arming to overthrow the " Constitution. However, this able man lays down " a few general principles, and gives a few facts, " which are of great value to me. His report came " to me from Rowan. My belief is, the Secretary " of State never saw it, nor the Horse Guards either; " it is worth their reading though!" " This Colonel " Shaw Kennedy, now a general, was the organiser " of the Irish constabulary; was one of Sir J. Moore's " men, and distinguished alike in peace and war by

" cool intrepidity, administrative talent, and com-
" manding decision of character."

I conclude this memoir by the relation of an
anecdote of the Duke of Wellington that I think
is of some importance. During the siege of Ciudad
Rodrigo, the Light Division was quartered at
Guinaldo, &c., and had therefore a march of some
eight or ten miles to make, and had to ford the
Agueda each time that it was taken forward to
the place. On the day preceding the night on which
the place was stormed, the division was ordered
forward to the place in the open daylight, consequently its movement was seen from the place.
After the division had commenced its march, General
Craufurd sent me forward to inform the Duke of
Wellington that the division was in march towards
the place, and requesting his Grace's instructions,
both as to the line of march to be followed by the
division upon approaching the place, and also as to
where and how the division was to form. I found
the Duke's staff near to the convent of St. Francisco,
and said I wished to see the Duke. They pointed
out the Duke sitting by himself under the shelter
of a wall, writing, and said that I could not speak to
him, as he was writing orders for the assault. I of
course paid no attention to this warning, but, going
directly up to the Duke, delivered General Craufurd's
message. He stopped writing, heard attentively the

message, gave clear and distinct answers to it and
instructions as to the march and formation of the
division, and after doing so resumed writing. Here,
then, we see this great man defer writing his instructions for the assault to the last moment, and writing
those instructions in the open air, within the fire of
the place, in a winter day, without engineer, staff
officer, or any documents to refer to, the whole being
evidently the pouring out of his own views and
determinations, and, as seen afterwards, written in
the most perspicuous and clear terms. His having
delayed the writing of the order to the last moment
was evidently with the view of its embracing every
circumstance that might occur, so as to comprehend
and provide for everything upon the circumstances
as they actually should stand when the assault was
given. This showed the confidence he had in his
own powers, and its having been done so well shows
that the subject was so thoroughly digested in his
own mind—he was so completely master of it in all
its general bearings and all its details—that he had
no difficulty in stating the order in a few clear and
well-arranged paragraphs. Here we arrive at the
same important result before alluded to, that great
commanders such as Cæsar, Wellington, and Napoleon, having their minds fully prepared by the study
of general principles, and combining that with some
experience, solve, on the instant, and in the midst of

the greatest turmoils of war, its most difficult and important problems; while commanders, unprepared by the careful study of principles, feel themselves in constant doubt and difficulty as new cases present themselves requiring altered arrangements to meet them, and those, in war, must be constant.

J. S. KENNEDY, Lieut.-General.

*Bath*, 8, *Circus*, *June*, 1860.

# NOTES

ON

# THE BATTLE OF WATERLOO.

# EXPLANATION AS TO THE SKETCHES.

IT is, of course, impossible to understand military operations without their description being illustrated by sketches showing the localities.

Accompanying these Notes will be found the following sketches :—

The plan of the battle of Waterloo, by Sergeant-Major Cotton, is given as showing very distinctly the two main ridges on which the French and Allied armies were formed; also the intermediate ridge, on which Napoleon placed his great battery of 74 pieces of artillery; and, as showing also clearly a small ridge which projects out nearly at right angles from the main ridge, from about where the Belgian Lion now stands : it shows also, pretty distinctly, the principal features of the ground towards Merbe-Braine. But the plans given in Captain Siborne's work are greatly superior for showing the positions of the troops.—

Ground-plan of the buildings of La Haye Sainte. (Page 94.)

Plan taken on the morning of the 19th of June, showing the position of the 3rd division in the action, and the peculiar formation which it adopted for resistance of the attacks of cavalry. (Page 99.)

Plan of Hougoumont. (Page 105.)

In addition to these, the reader is referred to the excellent Maps and Plans given by Captain Siborne * in his account of the battle.

---

* 'History of the War in France and Belgium in 1815.' By Captain W. Siborne. 2 vols. 8vo., with folio Atlas. Boone, Bond Street, 1844.

# NOTES ON THE BATTLE OF WATERLOO.

1. IN writing these Notes on the Battle of Waterloo, had I followed the dictates of my own taste and feelings, I should not have written even one sentence in the first person. The Notes may, or they may not, be interesting; that is not a point for me to determine; but it is certain that, if they do possess any interest, it must chiefly arise from the parts of the narration and remarks that are new being supported by personal observation, and by information obtained in the staff situation which I filled. It necessarily follows, that, to do justice to the subject, I must write to some extent in the first person; in fact, it is from the advantages and opportunities I had of knowing personally some important points of the action, which have not, I think, been hitherto fully described, that I have been induced to write these Notes; and the narrative and observations must, therefore, to show on what they rest, be occasionally personal.

2. It will be asked why any further account of the Waterloo campaign is required, as it has been so often

E

described ? To this question it is necessary that I should fully reply; for certainly, if the operation has already been fully explained, it must be a mere piece of impertinent supererogation to add to the numerous accounts already before the public.

3. I cannot, however, but think that the operation has not yet been described in such a way as to make it fully understood. Three writers on the subject were great masters in tactics and strategy,—that is, Wellington, Napoleon, and Jomini. Two of the three saw the battle, and can only be ranked with the greatest commanders who have ever lived. The third did not see the battle. As to Wellington's account of the battle, it was merely an official despatch, written in the hurry of the moment, to give the heads of the action and its result. Napoleon's account of the battle was dictated at St. Helena, and is in many respects of great value; but its unfairness, in some respects, I hold to be manifest. Jomini's account was written under the disadvantage of his not having seen the action; nor do I consider that he has made himself sufficiently master of the details and circumstances. His account is rather flippant and superficial.

4. Of the other writers on the subject, in none of them were combined the qualifications and opportunities necessary to enable them fully to describe the battle. But this sweeping objection must be modified

and explained in regard to one of the writers on the subject. Captain Siborne's account of the campaign has very great merit. I doubt if, as to any other battle, there ever were a greater number of facts brought together, or more care, industry, and fidelity displayed in their collection ; so that all other accounts of the battle, to be correct, must, for a great portion of the details, borrow from Siborne, as he had access to sources of information that no historian following him can have. In these Notes I have trusted to, and borrowed from him, the great body of the details. But Siborne fails in three respects : 1st, he was not well acquainted with the principles of the higher parts of war; 2nd, he failed to separate the salient points of the battle of Waterloo, and to show how the five acts into which that great drama was divided, produced the result by which the battle was decided; 3rd, he was led into misapprehensions as to the effects of the cavalry attacks ; and his views altogether respecting the cavalry attacks were erroneous and defective. In addition to these deficiencies, I am aware that, without its being in the slightest degree his fault, there were circumstances of importance on which he had not, and could not obtain, information.

5. But, even on the supposition that all the objections which I have made to the existing accounts of the battle are correct, still it remains for me to show

under what circumstances I can pretend to write on the subject with superior advantages to those who have already given accounts of this great historical event.

6. In the first place, I do not profess to write a full and formal history of the campaign of Waterloo, but merely an account of the battle of the 18th of June. What I intend these Notes to contain is an intelligible general account of the battle ;—a detailed account of the great cavalry attacks, and of the circumstances under which they were made, and of the previous arrangements which were made in anticipation of them by the 3rd division ;—a description of the ground, and a statement as to the numbers and force of the contending troops ;—with military criticisms on some parts of the battle, and the operations connected with it ;—and thus to form a supplementary work to the existing accounts, correcting some errors, enlarging the information which they give, and offering some views of the operations different from what have been given in former accounts.

7. The circumstances which have led me to the supposition that I am in a position to write Notes on the operations of Waterloo are the following :—1st. I was the only officer of the Quartermaster-General's Staff with the 3rd division of the army in the action : that division, consisting of six thousand men, occupied the very centre of the position, and from

the ground on which it stood the whole field of battle was well seen; and I examined, at the time, the ground both to the right and left of the division, and inspected the whole field some years afterwards. 2nd. The circumstances of the action brought me into personal contact, during its progress, with Generals Alten, Halkett, Maitland, and Kruse; and also with the Duke of Wellington, the Prince of Orange, the Quartermaster-General of the army, and the Deputy Quartermaster-General of the corps : and as my communications with them were upon important points of the action, I had the advantage of knowing their opinions on some points of it. And, 3rdly, I have the advantage of having seen and compared all the published accounts of the action up to this date (April, 1863), deriving from them such views and facts as seem legitimate. As regards the principles of war which were favourably exemplified by the operations, or violated by them, I may perhaps fail to convince my readers. I can only plead that to the discussion of such points I have paid long and earnest attention.

8. All the published accounts of the battle of Waterloo have, in my opinion, the defect of not separating the important portions of the action from each other. Without doing so the battle cannot, I conceive, be understood. The battle of Waterloo had this distinctive character, that it was divided into five

separate attacks ; four of which were isolated attacks, and one only, that is the last, was general on the whole Anglo-Allied line : those five attacks were distinct, and clearly separated from each other by periods of suspension of any close attacks. In fact, it can scarcely be said that figurative language is used in describing the action, by saying that the battle was a great drama in five acts, with distinct and well-defined intervals ; those intervals being marked simply by the firing of the batteries, without that fire being accompanied by any other action of the troops. This isolation of the attacks, as will be seen as the narrative progresses, was a matter of the greatest importance as regarded the result of the action; and the five great acts—that is, the five great attacks made by Napoleon—must be clearly classed in the mind of the reader, and distinctly separated from each other ; their time of commencement, their duration, and their comparative importance, must be marked and remembered. I shall, in narrating them, endeavour to put an approximative value on each of these great acts of the drama, estimating its effects upon the final issue of the contest.

9. There are certain points on which the reader must be informed before he can thoroughly understand an account of the battle of Waterloo ; previously, therefore, to entering upon the narrative, I shall describe the general features of the ground on which

the action was fought; the buildings and enclosures, the occupation of which became objects of attack and defence; I shall state the force of each of the antagonistic armies; and shall give the strength of the chief portions of each army that came separately in collision with each other; I shall state what was the general formation of each army in its order of battle; describing the peculiar formation of part of the Allied army to resist the attacks of the French cavalry; and pointing out the advantages and disadvantages of the defensive position of the Allies, both as regards the position itself, and the mode of occupying it. Even at the risk of being considered tedious, I shall describe all these points, in some detail, previous to entering on the account of the action itself. After these details are tolerably well mastered, the account of the fighting part can be easily and clearly understood, and fully appreciated. Readers who do not wish to study these details may pass on to section 95, where the account of the action begins.

10. The explanation of the formation of the 3rd division to resist cavalry, and of the circumstances which led to the adoption of that formation, may appear to be a digression; but it seems to me so important as to require a full explanation. As the great attack made by the French cavalry on the centre of Wellington's line was so important as to have a great influence on the result of the action, the reader should

be prepared by a previous explanation of the circumstances; as, without such previous explanation, he
could not fully understand the narrative.

11. Siborne says that the Duke of Wellington had
on the field of Waterloo :—

|  |  | Men. |
|---|---|---|
| Infantry | .. .. .. .. .. .. | 49,608 |
| Cavalry | .. .. .. .. .. .. | 12,408 |
| Artillery | .. .. .. .. .. .. | 5,645 |
| Grand total | .. .. .. | 67,661 |

And 156 guns.

And that Napoleon had,—

|  |  | Men. |
|---|---|---|
| Infantry | .. .. .. .. .. .. | 48,950 |
| Cavalry | .. .. .. .. .. .. | 15,765 |
| Artillery | .. .. .. .. .. .. | 7,232 |
| Grand total | .. .. .. | 71,947 |

And 246 guns.

Napoleon's 71,947 men were all old soldiers, and
all Frenchmen; Wellington's 67,661 men were made
up as follows, viz. :—

|  |  | Men. |
|---|---|---|
| British | .. .. .. .. .. .. .. | 23,991 |
| King's German Legion | .. .. .. | 5,824 |
| Hanoverians | .. .. .. .. .. | 11,247 |
| Brunswickers | .. .. .. .. .. | 5,935 |
| Nassauers | .. .. .. .. .. .. | 2,880 |
| Dutch-Belgians | .. .. .. .. .. | 17,784 |
| Total | .. .. .. .. | 67,661 |

12. But those who are contented with seeing
merely the bare numbers of the contending forces can

form no just idea what was really the comparative strength of the two armies. In order to form a just opinion on this point, it is necessary to know that the Dutch-Belgian troops, from political or other causes, which it is unnecessary to inquire into, would not fight the French ; and that of the other troops of the Duke of Wellington's force a portion were raw, recently raised, and imperfectly disciplined troops from various parts of Germany; while Napoleon's whole army were old soldiers, highly disciplined, and acting under a feeling of great excitement and enthusiasm. Taking the British troops and King's German Legion, as above, at 29,815 men, and allowing that the remainder of Wellington's force on the field was equal to 11,000 British troops, I estimate that Wellington fought with a force equal at the utmost to 41,000 British troops. It may be said that this is a fanciful estimate ; but it is not really so. I deduct, first, the part of the Dutch-Belgians who did not fight at all; and I could form a fair estimate of the value of the others, as compared with British troops.

13. From half-past eleven o'clock A.M. till six o'clock P.M. Wellington fought with a force highly estimated when stated to be equal to 41,000 British troops ; and during that period Napoleon fought with a force of, say, 61,000 excellent French troops.

14. After that hour the preponderance of force against Napoleon was very great ; but for two hours

longer Wellington's position was critical, from being closely in contact with so powerful a force, and that force acting with great energy and enthusiasm. The force opposing Blucher's attack acted with so much firmness and resolution as to hold its ground against greatly superior numbers. This prevented the necessity of Napoleon's withdrawing from the attack the troops which were in actual collision with those of Wellington; and proves with what admirable discipline and valour the French army fought.

15. Napoleon's force, with which he attacked Wellington from half-past eleven till six o'clock, I reduce from 71,947 men to 61,147 men. The infantry, cavalry, and artillery under Lobau, Danmont, and Subervie, formed in columns on the Genappe road, between La Haye Sainte and La Belle Alliance, before the action began, were, say, 10,820 men, and took no part whatever in the attack on Wellington's position in any part of the day : the cavalry of this force was sent early (about one o'clock) to oppose the Prussian advance ; and the infantry were kept as a reserve first, and afterwards supported the cavalry, so that it never acted against Wellington's line of battle. After six o'clock Napoleon was obliged to detach from the Guard also, to hold Planchenoit, and to check the other Prussian attacks in that direction. By seven o'clock twelve battalions of the Guard (one-half of all of the infantry of the Guard

that was with Napoleon) were employed in the defence of Planchenoit.

16. More detailed accounts of the ground and position will follow : it here seems only necessary to say, as a general description of the ground of the field of battle,[1] that a valley, commencing higher up than Hougoumont and the Nivelles road, continues down past La Haye Sainte, and from that to and below Smohain ; that all those three places were situated in this continuous hollow ; that the French army was drawn up in order of battle on the rising ground on one side of the valley, and the Allied army on the other ; that the field of battle was without enclosures of any kind, except those at the Château of Hougomont, the farm of La Haye Sainte, the hamlet of Smohain, the farm of Ter la Haye, and the farm of Papelotte ; that the ground on each side of the valley was of easy access, and of such a moderate ascent as to allow of charges of cavalry up it, at all points, at full gallop ; and that the ascent to reach the left of the line of battle of the Allies was longer, and in parts somewhat steeper, than the ground opposite to their centre and right, although not so high.

17. The Allied army took up its position as follows :—On the extreme left was Vivian's brigade of cavalry (the 6th British), consisting of the 10th and 18th British Hussars, and 1st Hussars of the King's

---

[1] See sketch, p. 105 ; also the plans in Captain Siborne's work.

German Legion. This brigade had a picket, consisting of a squadron of the 10th Hussars, in Smohain. The strength of the brigade was, say, 1244. The ground on its left afforded it no protection whatever; that is, the left of the army was in no way strengthened by the nature of the ground, and the country was perfectly open.

18. Upon Vivian's right was the cavalry brigade of Vandeleur, consisting of the 11th, 12th, and 16th Light Dragoons;—strength of the brigade (4th British), say, 1012.

19. The hamlet of Smohain, and the farms of La Haye and Papelotte, were occupied by the 2nd Dutch-Belgian division, commanded by General Perponcher; while the reserve of the division stood near to the summit of the slope above Papelotte, and near to and in front of the Wavre road. The division was 4300 strong.

20. On the main ridge of the position, behind the Wavre road, and on Vandeleur's right, stood the 5th Hanoverian brigade, under Colonel Von Vincke: this brigade, 2366 strong, belonged to Picton's division.

21. On the immediate right of Vincke's brigade stood the 4th Hanoverian brigade, under Colonel Best, 2582 strong. This brigade, which belonged to the 6th division, was drawn up close to the Wavre road, and its right rested upon a knoll that was the highest and most commanding point of that part of

the position occupied by the left wing of the Allied army.

22. Bylandt's brigade, of Perponcher's division, 3233 strong, was posted (most unaccountably as I conceive) in front of the Wavre road, on the slope on the right, and in advance of Best's brigade, and partly in direct front of Pack's brigade. In this position it was jutted forward in front of the real line of battle, which was mainly the Wavre road. It was directly exposed to the fire of the greatest French battery that was on the field, and singly exposed to the first onset of the French attacking columns.

23. To the right rear of Best's brigade stood Pack's brigade, being the 9th British brigade, and part of Picton's division. It consisted of the 3rd battalion 1st Royal Regiment, the 1st battalion 42nd Highlanders, the 2nd battalion 44th Regiment, and the 92nd Highlanders. The 44th Regiment, being the left battalion of the brigade, was placed on the knoll in rear of the right of Best's brigade, and the other three in columns at deploying distances, to the right of the 44th. The three right battalions of the brigade covered about half of the left of Bylandt's brigade, but were two hundred yards from the Wavre road, which also separated them. Why Bylandt's brigade was not withdrawn behind the Wavre road, and placed between Pack's and Kempt's brigades, remains,

so far as I know, unexplained. The strength of Pack's brigade was 1713.

24. The 8th British brigade, Picton's division, 1958 strong, commanded by Kempt, consisting of the 28th, 32nd, and 79th Regiments, and 1st battalion 95th Rifles, had its right on the Charleroi road, and its left extending towards Pack's right, but with a considerable interval between the brigades. The 32nd Regiment formed the right, and the 28th the left of this brigade. This brigade was placed nearer to the Wavre road than that of Pack. Three companies of the 95th occupied a knoll and sandpits at one hundred and twenty yards in front of the Wavre road; they were on the Charleroi road, nearly opposite to the garden of La Haye Sainte: the remaining companies of the battalion formed behind the Wavre road.

25. In continuation of the line of battle to the right, stood the 3rd division, under Count Alten, its left brigade, Ompteda's, 1527 strong, having its left on the Charleroi road; thus connecting the defence with the 32nd Regiment. On Ompteda's right was Kielmansegge's brigade, 3002 strong; and on Kielmansegge's right was Halkett's (the 5th British) brigade, 1782 strong. The right of this brigade extended to the right of where the Belgian Lion now stands. From Ompteda's brigade the 2nd light battalion of the King's German Legion, under Colonel

Baring, 400 strong, was detached to occupy La Haye
Sainte.

26. The 1st British division, under General Cooke,
was on the right of Halkett's brigade. Next to
Halkett's stood Maitland's brigade, 1582 strong, consisting of the 2nd and 3rd battalions of the 1st Regiment of Foot Guards.

27. Upon Maitland's right stood Byng, who commanded the 2nd brigade, composed of the 2nd
battalion of the 2nd or Coldstream Regiment, and
the 3rd battalion of the 3rd Regiment of Foot Guards;
strength, 1629 men. Maitland's and Byng's brigades
of Guards occupied the space between the right of
Halkett's brigade and the Nivelles road. Hougoumont was occupied by the four light companies of
the 1st division, the 1st battalion of the 1st Nassau
Regiment, a company of Hanoverian Riflemen, and a
detachment of a hundred men from the field battalion
Lunaberg, of Kielmansegge's brigade. To these
troops, occupying the buildings and enclosures of
Hougoumont, Byng's brigade of Guards stood in
support.

28. The 4th British brigade of the 4th division
(the two other brigades of the division being near
Hal, under Colville), 1767 strong, and composed of
the 3rd battalion 14th Regiment, 23rd Fusiliers, and
51st Light Infantry, occupied strongly, with a line of

skirmishers and pickets, the avenue leading from Hougoumont into the Nivelles road, and a portion of the road leading from that point towards Braine la Leud ; and the three battalions stood, in fact, in support of that advanced line ; two of the battalions on the right and one on the left of the Nivelles road. This line of posts was supported by a squadron of the 15th British Hussars ; and where it passed the Nivelles road, an abattis was thrown across that road. Colville's division, and the 2nd division under Clinton, formed the 2nd corps under Lord Hill.

29. A narrow road which leads from the point where the Hougoumont avenue joins the Nivelles road to the west side of Merbe Braine, following the line of the old Nivelles road, the Braine la Leud road, which runs in front of Merbe Braine to the Nivelles road, and part of the Nivelles road itself,— all run in hollow ways; and those three portions of road enclose a triangular space which forms a plateau of considerable strength. On this plateau stood the three brigades of Clinton's division. Du Plat's brigade, 1758 strong, stood in column parallel to, and with its left flank near to, the Nivelles road. Adam's brigade, 2621 strong, composed of the 52nd Light Infantry, the 71st Regiment, the 2nd battalion 95th Rifles, and two companies of the 3rd battalion 95th Rifles, stood in contiguous columns farther

back on the plateau; and Halkett's Hanoverian brigade, 2454 strong, stood still farther back, close to, and in front of, Merbe Braine.

30. This disposition of the troops, by which the right of the army was thrown back at right-angles to the right of the Guards, as the latter stood in line of battle behind Hougoumont, rendered the right of the Allied army almost unassailable, so long as the Guards should hold Hougoumont; for from Hougoumont to Merbe Braine a strong line of battle could be formed, which would have presented the following most formidable obstacles to Napoleon's making a great effort on the Allied right :—1st. The strength of the ground from Hougoumont to Merbe Braine, while the Allied army held both of those places. 2nd. That by such a movement Napoleon might have lost his communication with the Charleroi road. 3rd. That (as remains to be described) Wellington had considerable forces at Braine la Leud and Tubize, —the latter only 8½ miles distant,—by which the French attacking force might have been attacked in rear. And 4th. That by such an attack Napoleon would have left the junction of Wellington's and Blucher's forces altogether unmolested.

31. The troops on the plateau in front of Merbe Braine, if not attacked in that position, formed a reserve for the rest of the army, and especially to its right.

F

32. The whole of the cavalry of the Allied army, with the exception of Vivian's and Vandeleur's brigades, stood in rear of the line of battle formed by the infantry; and the high ground on which the infantry stood, sloping down to the north, gave such cover to the troops immediately in rear of the line of infantry, that the cavalry, although placed very near to the infantry, were not seen from the French position.

33. Beginning from the right, the Allied cavalry, with the exception of Vivian's and Vandeleur's brigades, stood as follows :—

34. The 5th brigade, under Grant, 1162 strong, consisting of the 7th and 15th Hussars and the 13th Light Dragoons. Grant's brigade consisted properly of the 7th and 15th Hussars, and 2nd Hussars King's German Legion. But the latter corps was left on the French frontier, and the 13th Light Dragoons, from Arentschildt's brigade, was attached to Grant's brigade. This brigade had its right resting on the Nivelles road, and stood behind the infantry brigades of Byng and Maitland. In rear of the brigade stood the Cumberland Hanoverian Hussars, 497 strong.

35. On Grant's left stood Dornberg's brigade, 1268 strong, consisting of the 23rd Light Dragoons and the 1st and 2nd Light Dragoons of the King's German Legion. This brigade stood behind Halkett's British brigade of infantry.

36. To Dornberg's left, and behind Kruse's infantry, stood the 3rd Hussars of the King's German Legion, 622 strong, under Arentschildt.

37. Lord Edward Somerset's brigade, 1226 strong, consisting of the 1st and 2nd Life Guards and the Royal Horse Guards (Blues) and the 1st Dragoon Guards, stood with its left resting on the Charleroi road, immediately in rear of the infantry brigades of Ompteda and Kielmansegge.

38. Ponsonby's brigade, 1181 strong, consisting of the 1st Dragoons (Royals), the 2nd Dragoons (Greys), and the 6th Dragoons (Inniskillings), stood on the left of the Charleroi road, in rear of the brigades of Kempt and Pack.

39. The reserve to Wellington's line of battle consisted of Collaert's division of cavalry, the Brunswick corps, and Lambert's brigade, the 10th British.

40. The Brunswick corps, 5452 strong, consisting of both cavalry and infantry, was posted with its left on the Nivelles road, and its right extended to Merbe Braine.

41. Collaert's division consisted of the brigades of Merlen, 1082 strong; Trip, 1337 strong; and Chigny, 1086 strong. Merlen and Trip stood between the Charleroi and Nivelles roads, on the immediate right of the farm of Mont St. Jean; and Chigny's brigade was on the left of the Charleroi road, with its right resting on the farm of Mont St. Jean.

42. Lambert's brigade, 2182 strong, composed of the 4th, 27th, and 46th Regiments, only arrived on the ground after the commencement of the action, and was at first posted behind the farm of Mont St. Jean, but afterwards advanced to the right of Kempt's brigade and rested its right on the Charleroi road.

43. Wellington's line of battle may be considered as having extended one mile to the right, and one mile to the left, of the point where the road from Wavre crosses the great Charleroi road, being on the summit of the ridge, and following very nearly the line of the Wavre road. The position was good, and was strongly and well occupied; but the occupation does not set criticism at defiance. Bylandt's brigade, as already mentioned, was badly placed; La Haye Sainte was not so strongly occupied as it ought to have been; and the deficiency of reserves was so great that Colville's two brigades should have been sent for at ten o'clock A.M. The directions to these brigades should have been, that they were to march directly to the field of battle, if they had no enemy in their front. This would have been a perfectly safe order, and, had it been given, the two brigades would have been on the field of battle between two and three o'clock. There would have remained still on the Hal road 11,157 men, under the Prince Frederick of Orange, covering the road to Brussels;

Braine la Leud was occupied by the 3rd division of the Netherlands, under Baron Chassé, 6669 strong; so that the right of the Allied army was perfectly secured, and no enemy was heard of on the Hal road by the pickets who, no doubt, patrolled the roads many miles to their front.

44. It is difficult to understand how any fear of the Hal road could have existed up to ten o'clock on the morning of the 18th June. Upon an examination of the map, and on a careful consideration of the circumstances, it will be difficult to comprehend how any French force could have got to Tubize and Hal without its advance being long previously known. Such force must have marched either by Mons or Nivelles, which, independently of the information by the military patrols and posts, would have spread general alarm along the line of those two great roads leading to Brussels. Colville's division (with the exception of the 4th brigade) had passed the night of the 17th at Braine le Comte, only marching on the morning of the 18th to Tubize ;[1] so that, if any French force had passed Mons, Colville must have known it, and the roads were, of course, patrolled to Nivelles and towards the great Char-

---

[1] Colville's division was 5445 strong; the 4th brigade was 1767 strong: so that the force under Colville detained at Tubize, which might have joined Wellington, consisted of 3678 men.

leroi road. That Napoleon would detach a force by either the Mons or Nivelles road was not to be apprehended; if he had sent a large force, his doing so would have weakened his line of battle, and sending a small force would have been to ensure its destruction.

45. In order to understand the position taken up by Wellington, it is necessary to know what the ground-plans were of the buildings at the Château of Hougoumont and the Farm of La Haye Sainte, and also what the enclosures were at each of them. This no mere verbal description can give in a way that is satisfactory to the mind, but it is seen and understood sufficiently upon a very slight inspection of Plans: such as that of La Haye Sainte (p. 94), and the plan of Hougoumont (p. 105).

46. From the great solidity of the buildings of La Haye Sainte; from those buildings, together with the high wall along the Charleroi road, forming a complete enclosure of very strong masonry; and from the great space afforded by the buildings and the large court enclosed by them,—it is at once obvious and certain that those buildings could, in the course of a night, have been rendered so strong that, had they been properly occupied (that is, garrisoned sufficiently), and proper defensive measures adopted, there would have been scarcely a possibility of their falling into the hands of the enemy. But they

did fall into the hands of the enemy; and their having done so will be shown, as this narrative progresses, to have greatly endangered the success of the Allied army. The garrison was insufficient, the workmen were taken away, the place was declared to be sufficiently strong for all that was wanted of it, and nothing whatever was done during the night towards its defence; in place of which, the works of scaffolding, loopholing, building up gates and doors, partial unroofing, throwing out the hay and securing a supply of ammunition, should have been in progress all the night and during the morning. The impracticable attempt of defending the orchard and garden of La Haye Sainte was made, which ended — and only could end—in the defeat of, and great loss to, the defenders; these enclosures were merely hedges, and they were exposed to the immediate attacks of the centre—that is, the greatest force of the French army—and to the fire of 74 French guns that were posted within range of them. It will be seen from measurements given in the ground-plan that the buildings, and court enclosed by the buildings, and wall along the road, were capable of holding a garrison of 1000 men.

47. The buildings at Hougoumont were also of substantial masonry, and capable of a good defence. The garden, being enclosed on the south and east by a wall of masonry, made it also a very important post. The

defence of Hougoumont had been looked upon in a different light from that of La Haye Sainte. Intimation was given on the evening of the 17th that it was to be defended to the utmost; the workmen and tools from La Haye Sainte were sent to it; an additional supply of ammunition was placed in it; and the works of loopholing and preparing platforms were carried on with energy.

48. The artillery of the Anglo-Allied army was posted as follows :—Gardiner's troop, 6 guns, 6-pounders, with Vivian's brigade; battery of 8 guns, under Captain Byleveld, Dutch-Belgians, with Perponchier's division. On the highest point of the position (already mentioned), Captain Von Rettberg's Hanoverian brigade, 6 guns, 9-pounders; with Kempt's, Major Rogers' British brigade, 6 guns, 9-pounders; with Alten's division, Major Lloyd's British, and Major Cleeves's King's German brigades, each 6 guns, 9-pounders; with Cooke, Major Kiehlmann's troop of Hanoverian, and Captain Sandham's brigade of British, each 6 guns, 9-pounders; with Clinton, Major Sympher's King's German troop, and Captain Bolton's brigade, 6 guns each, 9-pounders. The other troops of horse-artillery, each troop having 5 guns, 9-pounders, were with the cavalry : viz. Major Bull's; Lieut.-Colonel W. Smith's; Major Whingate's (provided with rockets); Captain Mercer's and Major Ramsay's; Captain Petter's Dutch-Belgian

troop of 8 guns was with Collaert. Captain Van der Smissen's troop of 8 guns, and Captain Lux's brigade of 8 guns, were with Chassé. The Brunswick troop under Captain Heinemann, and a brigade under Major Moll, of 8 guns each, were with the Brunswick corps. The British troop under Major Beane, and the brigade under Captain Sinclair, the Hanoverian brigade under Captain Braun, and the troop under Ross, each having 5 guns, 9-pounders, formed the reserve. The whole of the artillery was brought forward during the action; Ross's troop was placed near to where the Wavre and Charleroi roads cross each other, two of the guns being placed on the Charleroi road.

49. It must be borne in mind that the troops under the Prince Frederick of Orange at Hal, and the two brigades under Colville at Tubize, are not included in the 67,661 men that the Duke of Wellington had on the field of battle; but Chassé's force, which occupied Braine la Leud, and the ground in its vicinity, for the purposes of strengthening Wellington's right, and keeping open the communication with Tubize, did form part of the 67,661 men.

50. The movement of the French army, by which it was formed in order of battle, immediately opposite to and in preparation for attacking the Allied army, was executed by a very simple and ably-conceived movement of the whole army in eleven columns, each

column marching directly to, and occupying, the ground on which it was to stand. The result of the movement was the formation of a line of battle so skilfully arranged that it may be looked upon as a model. It consisted of two lines of infantry; two lines of heavy cavalry; a reserve of infantry and cavalry, in column, behind the centre; and the great reserve of the army (the infantry of the Imperial Guard) in close contiguous columns, still farther in rear of the centre. The two front lines of infantry, and two lines of heavy cavalry, stood in contiguous columns, but occupied sufficient space to deploy upon. The movement of Napoleon's army, by which it took up its position in order of battle, was to those on the Anglo-Allied position who witnessed it highly interesting, and, as a sight, majestic and beautiful.

51. The following description of the formation of the French army, given from paragraph 52 to paragraph 69, was dictated by Napoleon himself, when at St. Helena :—

52. " At eight o'clock on the morning of June 18th, " 1815, the Emperor's breakfast was served, at which " several General Officers were present : the Emperor " said, ' The enemy's army is superior in numbers to " ours by at least one-fourth; nevertheless we have " at least ninety chances in our favour, and not ten " against us.' ' Without doubt,' replied Marshal Ney, " who entered the tent at this moment, ' if the Duke

" of Wellington were simple enough to wait for your
" Majesty; but I am come to announce that already
" his columns are in full retreat, and disappearing
" in the forest.' 'You are mistaken,' replied the
" Emperor; ' he is no longer in time; he would ex-
" pose himself to certain destruction : the dice have
" been thrown, and the chances are in our favour.'

53. " Some artillery officers who had been ex-
" ploring the plain now announced .that the artillery
" could manœuvre, though under some difficulties,
" which would be sensibly diminished in an hour.
" The Emperor immediately mounted his horse, rode
" towards the riflemen stationed opposite to La Haye
" Sainte, reconnoitred anew the enemy's line, and
" charged the General de Génie Haxo—an officer
" in his confidence—to approach still nearer, and
" ascertain if any redoubts or intrenchments had been
" raised. The General speedily returned, and re-
" ported that he could perceive no traces whatever
" of field-works. The Emperor reflected a quarter
" of an hour, and then dictated the order of battle,
" which two generals wrote while seated on the
" ground.

54. " The Aides-de-Camp took the orders to the
" different corps d'armée, who were under arms, and
" full of impatience and ardour. The army pre-
" pared for action, and marched forward in eleven
" columns.

55. "These eleven columns were designed,—four
" to form the 1st line, four to form the 2nd line, and
" three to form the 3rd line. The four columns of
" the 1st line were,—

" 1st. That on the left, comprising the cavalry of
" the 2nd corps.

" 2nd. Three divisions of infantry, forming the
" 2nd corps.

" 3rd. Four divisions of infantry, forming the 1st
" corps.

" 4th. The light cavalry of the 1st corps.

56. " The four columns of the 2nd line were,—

" 1st. That on the left, formed by Kellermann's
" cuirassiers.

" 2nd. Two divisions of infantry, from the 6th
" corps.

" 3rd. Two divisions of light cavalry : one from
" the 6th corps, commanded by General Daumont;
" the other a detachment from the corps under Pajol,
" commanded by General Subervie.

" 4th. Milhaud's corps of cuirassiers.

57. " The three columns of the 3rd line were,—

" 1st. That on the left, formed by the division of
" horse-grenadiers and dragoons of the Guard, under
" General Guyot.

" 2nd. The three divisions of the Old, Middle, and
" Young Guard, under Lieutenant-Generals Friant,
" Morand, and Duhesme.

" 3rd. The Chasseurs à Cheval and the Lancers of
" the Guard, under Lieutenant-General Lefebvre-Des-
" nouettes. The artillery marched on the flanks of
" the columns; the parks and flying artillery formed
" the rear.

58. " At nine o'clock the heads of the four columns,
" forming the 1st line, arrived at the spot where they
" were to deploy. At the same time were seen,
" at various distances, the seven other columns de-
" scending from the heights. They were in full
" march; the trumpets and drums sounded over the
" field; the music re-echoed airs which recalled to
" the soldiers the remembrance of a hundred vic-
" tories; the earth seemed proud to bear so many
" brave men. The whole formed a magnificent spec-
" tacle, and must have struck the enemy with awe,
" who were so placed as to perceive every man, and
" to whom the army must have appeared double its
" real numbers.

59. " These eleven columns deployed not only
" without confusion, but with such accuracy that
" each man filled at once the place designed him by
" the Commander-in-Chief. Never had such masses
" moved with so much facility.

" The light cavalry of the 2nd corps, which formed
" the first column on the left of the 1st line, de-
" ployed in three ranks on either side of the road
" between Nivelles and Brussels, nearly as high as

" the outskirts of the park of Hougoumont, com-
" manding on the left all the plain, and having its
" main guards placed on Braine la Leud, its battery
" of light artillery on the road to Nivelles. The
" 2nd corps, under General Reille, occupied the
" space between the roads of Nivelles and Charleroi,
" covering an extent of from 5000 to 6000 feet.

60. " Prince Jerome's division was stationed on
" the left, near the road to Nivelles and the wood of
" Hougoumont; General Foy held the centre, and
" General Bachelu the right, reaching as far as the
" road to Charleroi, near to the farm of La Belle
" Alliance. Each division of infantry deployed in
" two lines, with an interval of 180 feet between
" them, having its artillery in front and its parks in
" the rear near the road to Nivelles.

61. " The 3rd column, formed by the 1st corps
" and commanded by Count d'Erlon, had on its left
" La Belle Alliance, on the right of the road to
" Charleroi; and its right opposite the farm of La
" Haye, which was held by a strong detachment
" from the left wing of the enemy. Each division
" of its infantry deployed in two lines, its artil-
" lery being stationed in the intervals between the
" brigades. Its light cavalry, which formed the
" 4th column, deployed on its right in three lines,
" commanding La Haye and Frischermont, and with
" its outposts overlooking Ohain to observe the

" flankers of the enemy, and its light artillery was
" on the right.

62. " The 1st line was scarcely formed when the
" heads of the four columns of the 2nd line arrived
" at the point from which they were to deploy.
" Kellermann's cuirassiers established themselves in
" two lines, with an interval of 180 feet between
" them, and at a distance of 600 feet from the 2nd
" line of the 2nd corps; having on their left the road
" to Nivelles, and their right extending as far as the
" road to Charleroi. The whole space occupied by
" them was about 6600 feet; one of their batteries
" took up its position on the left, near the road to
" Nivelles, the other on the right, near the road to
" Charleroi. The 2nd column, commanded by Lieu-
" tenant-General Count de Lobau, placed itself 300
" feet behind the 2nd line of the 2nd corps; it
" remained in column, compressed into two divisions,
" occupying a space of about 600 feet along and on
" the left of the road to Charleroi, with an interval
" of 60 feet between the two divisions, and having
" its artillery on its left flank.

63. " The 3rd column—that of its light cavalry,
" commanded by General Daumont, and followed
" by the division under General Subervie—disposed
" itself in close column of squadrons, having on its
" left the road to Charleroi, and opposite its infantry,
" from which it was separated only by that road; its

" light artillery was stationed on its right flank. The
" 4th column—that of Milhaud's corps of cuirassiers—
" deployed in two lines, with an interval of 180 feet
" between them, and 600 feet behind the 2nd line of
" the 1st corps ; having on the left the road to Char-
" leroi, and its right in the direction of Frischermont.
" This column occupied an extent of about 5400 feet ;
" its batteries were disposed in the centre, and on the
" left near the road to Charleroi.

64. " Before this 2nd line was fully formed the
" heads of the three columns of the reserve arrived at
" their points of deployment ; the heavy cavalry of
" the Guard was stationed at a distance of 600 feet
" behind Kellermann's cuirassiers. It deployed in
" two lines, with an interval of 180 feet between them,
" having the road to Nivelles towards the left, the
" road to Charleroi on the right, with its artillery in
" the centre.

65. " The centre column—formed by the infantry
" of the Guard—deployed in six lines of 4 battalions
" each, with intervals of 60 feet between the ranks,
" on either side the road to Charleroi, and somewhat
" in front of the farm of Rossomme.

66. " The artillery batteries belonging to the dif-
" ferent regiments were placed on the right, and on
" the left ; the horse and foot artillery of the reserve
" behind the ranks.

67. " The 3rd column—formed by the Chasseurs

" à Cheval, and the Lancers of the Guard—deployed
" in two lines, with an interval of 180 feet between
" them, and 600 feet behind Milhaud's cuirassiers,
" having on its left the road to Charleroi, its right
" extending towards Frischermont, and with the light
" artillery in the centre.

68. " At half-past ten o'clock, incredible though it
" may appear, the whole movement was completed,
" and all the troops were in their destined positions.
" The most profound silence pervaded the whole battle-
" field.

69. " The army was ranged in six lines, forming
" six double Ws. The 1st and 2nd lines were formed
" of infantry, and flanked by light cavalry ; the 3rd
" and 4th lines of cuirassiers; the 5th and 6th lines
" of cavalry of the Guard ; with six lines of infantry
" of the Guard perpendicularly placed at the point of
" these six Ws; and the 6th corps—compressed as
" a column—was placed perpendicularly to the lines
" occupied by the Guard : its infantry was on the
" left, and its cavalry on the right of the road. The
" roads to Charleroi and Nivelles were left free, as
" the means of communication by which the artillery
" of the reserve could reach with speed the various
" points of the line."[1]

---

[1] Paragraphs 52 to 69 cannot be fully understood without an
inspection of Captain Siborne's plan showing how the armies
stood before the battle commenced.

70. The following is given as an approximative estimate of the strength of the French divisions in the action of the 18th June, independent of the artillery. It may be estimated that a battery of 8 guns was with each division of infantry; and a battery of 6 guns with each division of cavalry; the average number of men with each battery being about 260. The strength of brigades for the Allied army, and that of divisions for the French army, are given, and will be found for each brigade of the Anglo-Allied force, and for each division of the French force, in Captain Siborne's plan. In the description of the action the details chiefly refer to brigades of the Allied force, and to divisions of the French force; so that the strength of the parts acting immediately against each other are best seen by this mode of stating the strength; by giving the strength of each British brigade, and of each French division, on the plan, the strengths of the contending portions of the hostile armies is made obvious.

71. The force under Lobau and Daumont, massed in columns of infantry and cavalry on each side of the Charleroi road, in support of the centre of the French line of battle, may be estimated at about 7460 infantry and artillery, and 3100 cavalry; making a total force of 10,560 men. Of this force no portion ever came into contact with the Anglo-Allied line, as the cavalry moved early in the day to oppose the

Prussian advance, and the infantry first remained as a support against the Prussian attack, and ultimately marched to meet that attack.

72. Beginning with the right of the French line of battle : Jaquinot's division had 11 squadrons, say 1400 strong, and a horse-battery, say 300 strong; in all, 1700 men.

73. The strength of each French division cannot be stated accurately ; but a sufficiently near approximation can be made. To ascertain the strength of each of the seven divisions forming the corps of D'Erlon and Reille, the safest and most intelligible mode is that of taking their average strength, by dividing the whole strength of D'Erlon's corps by four, and the whole strength of Reille's corps by three, making considerable allowance for the loss suffered by Reille's corps at Quatre Bras. This gives the following as the strength of the seven divisions :— Durutte 5000, Marcognet 5000, Alix 5000, Donzelot 5000, Bachelu 6000, Foy 6000, Prince Jérome Napoleon 6000; this being in succession the order in which those divisions stood in line from the right to the left of the line of battle. The division which formed the left of this front line of battle was the cavalry division of Piré, 1865 strong, with a horse battery of artillery.

74. The strength of the divisions of heavy cavalry, forming the second line of the French order of battle,

was as follows : the divisions are named from right to left of the line as they stood in succession in the order of battle :—Wautier 1886, Delort 1414, Lefebvre-Desnouettes 2000, L'Héritier 1650, Roussel 1650, and Guyot 2000 ; together with, say, 1400 artillery : in all 12,000 men.

75. The strength of the 24 battalions of the infantry of the Guard, placed in front of Rossomme, and forming the third line of the order of battle, was 12,000 ; that is, 500 per battalion, and 1800 artillery.

76. The right of the French army rested on Frischermont ; its centre was on the Charleroi road, at La Belle Alliance and Trimotion ; its left extended a short way beyond the Nivelles road, that is, on the Braine la Leud side of the Nivelles road.

77. The right wing of the French army, extending from the Charleroi road at La Belle Alliance to Frischermont, occupied a front of about one and one-eighth of an English mile, upon a ridge that extended between those two places, nearly parallel to the left wing of the Allied line of battle, and about 1400 yards distant from it, measuring from the front of La Belle Alliance to what was called the Wellington Tree, which stood in the angle (see Map at end) formed by the crossing of the Charleroi and Wavre roads—the point at which the left of the 3rd division rested. The left wing of the French army (extending from Trimotion to beyond the Nivelles road)

occupied a front of one English mile and a quarter ;
following nearly the line of the road from Planchenoit to Braine la Leud : for about the first half-mile
it sank down into the valley that separated the two
armies, but after that it continued on the ridge which
was within three or four hundred yards from the
enclosures of Hougoumont; and at that distance from
its enclosures, and about 500 yards from the buildings, partly swept round the south and west of Hougoumont. It seems unnecessary to describe further
the two main ridges on which Wellington's and
Napoleon's armies stood opposed to each other at
eleven o'clock A.M. on the 18th of June, for the line
of those ridges is best marked by the front lines of
their respective orders of battle, as shown in Captain
Siborne's plan.

78. As already stated in the general description of
the ground on which the contending armies stood,
and on which they fought, they were, when placed
in order of battle at eleven o'clock A.M., separated
from each other by a valley (see paragraph 16); but
this general valley had within it rises of ground,
without a knowledge of which, and of the uses that
could be and were made of them in the progress of
the action, some most important points of the action
cannot be understood : I therefore proceed to notice
the chief rise, and its spurs, that interrupted the

uniformity of the low ground that separated the two armies.

79. It extended from La Belle Alliance to where the Belgian Lion now stands, in a north-west direction, in the line marked A B C (Map at end);—and from the wood of Hougoumont in a north-easterly direction to within 700 yards of the farm of Papelotte, in a line marked D E F on the Map. It will be seen by the Map, that the parts on the lines from B to C, and from E to F, were spurs from the more extended part; those spurs were in some places nearly of the same height as the ground forming the main ridge on which the Anglo-Allied army stood: the highest part of the position of the Anglo-Allied army being the ground on which the 3rd division stood to the right rear of La Haye Sainte, which was 150 feet higher than the ground at Smohain.

80. A very slight degree of consideration will show the immense importance of those two spurs of rising ground. They so embraced La Haye Sainte as to come close to its orchard at the point where the Charleroi road reaches the orchard. On the spur which is on the east of that road, including a small extent to the west of the road, a battery of 74 French guns, consisting of 8 and 12 pounders, and howitzers, was established. This great battery was advanced to within 250 yards of the buildings of La Haye Sainte,

and to a distance of about 600 yards from the Wellington Tree, at the point of junction of the Charleroi and Wavre roads; being an auxiliary power of the highest importance for the objects of taking La Haye Sainte and breaking the centre of the line of battle of the Anglo-Allied army. The other spur—that which joined the main ridge about where the Belgian Lion now stands, and was nearly equidistant from the enclosures of Hougoumont and La Haye Sainte—was an approach to the main position of the Allies, and became important in the three last attacks on Wellington's line.

81. The valley which passes to the south of Hougoumont branches abruptly to the north, and continues to Merbe Braine, and its course is marked by the crossroad which runs along the lowest part of it from the end of the Hougoumont approach on the Nivelles road to Merbe Braine; and from this ravine runs another past Merbe Braine towards the Nivelles road; thus forming a sort of natural citadel of ground, on which Wellington could, and did, throw back his right, and which he most judiciously held as a security for his right, or as a position for a reserve force of infantry, to be used as the circumstances of the battle might indicate. By this excellent disposition Wellington quite secured his right, which he strengthened still further by occupying Braine la Leud with a very considerable force; which occupation also had the

effect of keeping up the communication with Tubize
and Hal.

82. The non-military reader should be informed,
so as to be able to judge of the manner in which
Wellington and Napoleon occupied their respective
positions at Waterloo, that 3000 infantry, or 1760
cavalry, drawn up in a single rank, occupy one
English mile of front; that is, each infantry soldier
occupies 21 inches of front, and each horse 36 inches
of front: consequently, when British infantry occupy,
in two lines, that is in four ranks, a field of battle
extending one mile in front, 11,200 men are required,
and a fourth of the whole infantry, all the cavalry,
and part of the artillery should be in reserve; so that
to occupy a position properly requires 20,000 troops
for each mile of front. Now, supposing that Wellington's and Napoleon's fronts of battle each extended
over two miles and a half, they would require 50,000
men each to occupy the ground as a field of battle;
and this at once shows conclusively that each of those
great commanders occupied his position very strongly.
The distance between the enclosures of Hougoumont
and La Haye Sainte is 1000 yards; this may be stated
as an instance of the necessity, in order to understand
the narrative of a battle, of knowing something of
the front that troops occupy. It was on this front
of 1000 yards that the great charges of the French
cavalry were made, consequently 1000 horsemen

would have filled the whole of it; which proves that
not more than, say, 500 men, could ever have been in
their front line, as they had to keep at some distance
\from the fire of both Hougoumont and La Haye
Sainte, and they charged with intervals: 12,000
cavalry, therefore, on this front, might charge in
twenty-four successive lines, supposing each line to
be a single rank.

83. The possession of Hougoumont and La Haye
Sainte was of such vital importance as regards the
result of the action, that it is necessary to give such
an account of them as will show the defensive capabilities of each.

84. The general enclosure of Hougoumont was a
quadrangle, the enclosure being a hedge, and the four
sides of nearly equal length, that is about 1700 feet
each; the eastern side was nearly parallel to the
Charleroi road; the northern side faced the right of
the Allied position; the southern and western sides
were opposite to the French position, which curved
round those two sides. An avenue of 700 feet in
length led from the Nivelles road to the north-west
angle of this enclosure, communicating with the
buildings. The great enclosure had within it the following subordinate enclosures, viz.—the south-western
portion was a wood; the south-eastern portion was
two open fields: these three enclosures occupied
more than half of the whole space that was within the

great outer enclosure.   Immediately north of the two open fields was a large orchard, while a small orchard stood immediately north of the wood, and formed a narrow stripe between it and the garden.   There was another small orchard immediately north of the garden, and a third orchard on the west of the wood. The garden was enclosed on the south and east sides by walls of masonry in brick.   These walls were loopholed by the British, and benches were placed behind them, which enabled the defenders to fire both through and over these walls.   These works were executed during the night of the 17th and morning of the 18th.   The buildings of the château and farm formed the western enclosures of the garden, and a hedge its northern enclosure.   The buildings formed two enclosed courts.   The château stood between the two courts : it fronted to the south and looked into the south court, the north court being behind it.   The château thus formed the northern enclosure of the one, and the southern enclosure of the other court.   The east side of the north court was enclosed by the farmhouse, cowhouses, and stabling, which separated it from the garden.   In the angle between the château and the farmhouse was a tower of the same height as the château, and forming a staircase to it ; and at the south-east corner and attached to it was a small chapel.   The enclosure of the north court was a continuation of the stabling, and a gateway which formed

the entrance from the avenue that led to the Nivelles
road. This gateway was not closed up, as it fronted
to the Allied position, and was kept as the communication with it : the other gateways were blocked up.
A large barn and shed formed the western enclosure
of the north court. What is here called the north
court was the farmyard. As already stated, the
château formed the north enclosure of the south court ;
its west enclosure was a continuation of the barn and
shed, and a gateway that gave access to the avenue
and Nivelles road, and to two roads which traversed
the wood and led into the cross road, which, leaving
the Charleroi road about 150 yards south of Trimotion, joins the Nivelles road about 550 yards south
of Hougoumont. Its east enclosure was a wall that
separated it from the garden : its south enclosure
was the gardener's houses and some out-door offices.
There were two means of communication between the
north and south courts : one by a doorway in a small
wall that joined the château and the barn, and another
through the barn. In the northern court there was
a well, surmounted by a dovecote. The whole length
of the buildings from north to south was about
280 feet, and their breadth from east to west about
150 feet. It will be found, when that part of the
narrative of the action is arrived at, that it is of
importance, for understanding the defence of Hougoumont, to recollect that the brick wall forming the

southern enclosure of the garden was about 600 feet
in length; that the brick wall which formed its
eastern enclosure was about 300 feet in length; and
that the northern enclosure of the large orchard, from
that point of it which would have been intersected by
a prolongation of the eastern garden-wall to its
north-eastern extremity, was about 800 feet.   It was
by holding these three lines of defence firmly during
the whole action, that the permanent possession of
the garden and the general possession of the orchard
were secured.   The occupation of the eastern garden-
wall, and of the northern enclosure of the orchard,
gave the defenders the advantage of a direct cross-
fire upon the orchard.

85. As already stated, the general valley separating
the hostile armies swept round the southern and
western enclosures of Hougoumont.   The enclosures
of Hougoumont were partly in the general valley that
separated the hostile armies, and partly on the western
end of the intermediate height, already described,
which rose in that general valley.   The highest part
of the enclosures was the eastern portion of the two
open fields that were on the east of the wood—part
of that enclosure being nearly equal in height to the
main position of the Anglo-Allied army.

86. The enclosures of Hougoumont, with the exception of those formed by the buildings, and by the
brick walls which formed the southern and eastern

enclosures of the garden, were hedges; and it is important to recollect (as they were points of serious contest) that the enclosures of the large orchard, on its north and south sides, were strong hedges, with ditches outside a portion of them.

87. The farmhouse of La Haye Sainte stood immediately on the west side of the Charleroi road. The house and offices formed the north, west, and south sides of a quadrangle; the east side being a high wall along the edge of the Charleroi road; the interior of the quadrangle formed the farmyard. On the south of the buildings was an orchard extending about 700 feet in length along the west side of the Charleroi road; it was 230 feet wide. The garden was on the north of the buildings, and was a square of 200 feet. The enclosures of the orchard and garden were hedges. (For ground-plan of La Haye Sainte, see p. 94.) From the northern side of the buildings to the Wellington Tree, or in other words from the farmhouse to the intersection of the Charleroi and Wavre roads, the distance was about 750 feet. The buildings of La Haye Sainte, which formed the north and west sides of the quadrangle, consisted of the farmhouse, stable, and cow-houses, forming one continuous building, the east end of the dwelling-house being next to the Charleroi road. The south side of the quadrangle consisted chiefly of a barn, the prolongation of its southern wall, till it

joined the high wall along the Charleroi road, forming the remainder of the southern enclosure of this quadrangle. The south-west angle, formed by the cowhouses and the barn, was filled up by a passage, which was entered by a large gateway. This passage, and the

GROUND-PLAN OF THE FARM OF LA HAYE SAINTE.

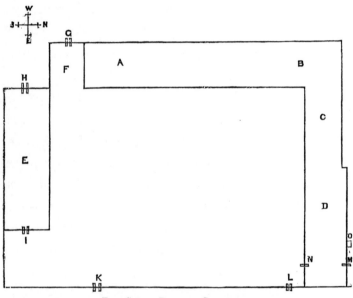

THE GREAT ROAD TO CHARLEROI.

A, B, C, D. Dwelling-house, stables, and cow-house, of which D is the dwelling-house.

  E. A barn.
  F. A passage.
  G. A great gate.
  H. A great gate.
  I. A door.
  K. A great gate.
  L, M, N. Doors.
  O. A well, being a square building, with loopholes flanking the door and wall.

The interior measure of the yard, from the building C D to the building E, is 40 yards, and 45 yards from the building A B to the wall K L.

The buildings are very strongly roofed and built. The passage F has the same roofing as the houses.

dwelling-house and offices, were all of good masonry, and strongly and well roofed. A large gateway led from the farmyard into the Charleroi road, through the high wall which formed the eastern enclosure of the quadrangle; this gateway was near to the south end of the farmyard. Very near to the dwelling-house there was also a doorway through the wall forming the eastern enclosure of the quadrangle, which communicated with the Charleroi road, and was near to the front door of the dwelling-house inside of the farmyard. The dwelling-house fronted into the farmyard. There was also a small door in the back of the dwelling-house, which led into the garden, and which immediately faced the Allied position. Whether there was a doorway at the back of the farmhouse leading into the garden, and so to the Allied position, was a matter of importance; and it is positively stated in most accounts of the action that there was no such door. Lord Ellesmere, who was in the most intimate and close communication with the Duke of Wellington on the subject when he wrote the two articles for the 'Quarterly Review' respecting the Campaign of Waterloo, would not admit the existence of this doorway; and Lord Fitzroy Somerset was determinedly of the same opinion. Thus the best authority seemed to prove that there was not a doorway communicating from the dwelling-house into the garden of La Haye Sainte, and so with the Allied posi-

tion; yet that doorway did exist; and, curiously
enough, it was, as if by design, flanked by a small
projecting square building very near to it, which pro-
jection was built to enclose a well, and in it were
openings that served as loopholes. What I now state
on the subject is from positive personal knowledge;
and what I have said as to Lord Ellesmere's and Lord
Fitzroy Somerset's opinions is the result of conversa-
tions which I had with them on the subject; that
with the latter about ten years ago; that with the
former took place two or three years before his death,
when he was in Bath. The whole of the masonry
enclosures of La Haye Sainte will be sufficiently
understood by reference to Sketch (p. 94), where
the ground-plan of the buildings is given: the enclosures of the garden and orchard were hedges.

88. The other enclosures occupied as part of the
line of battle of the Anglo-Allied army were, the
farm of Papelotte, the farm of La Haye, and the hamlet of Smohain. The two former were on the left of
the rivulet of Smohain, the latter on both sides of
that rivulet, which in fact had its rise very near to
Papelotte. Those places were not strengthened by
any works.

89. The plans of the battle given in Siborne's
work show sufficiently the general arrangement of
the troops of the Allied, French, and Prussian armies
on the field of battle; but I consider that the plan of

the battle which shows most clearly the general features of the ground is that which accompanies Sergeant-Major Cotton's account of the battle. (See Map at the end.) It can only be trusted to for the general features, but shows well the chief great undulation in the general valley that separated the main positions of the two armies. For the position of the troops Siborne's plans are much better; and for the ground the best seems Craan's, which I do not give.

90. The object of all the preceding paragraphs is that of giving to the reader, whether military or non-military, such information as will enable him easily to understand the narrative of the action. Not only will those preliminary explanations be absolutely necessary to enable the general reader fully to understand the battle, but, by clearing the ground completely before the narrative of the battle itself is entered upon, that narrative may be made very short and simple, while clearly pointing out the five great acts of the drama—which becomes impossible when the narrative is constantly interrupted and mixed up with explanations and references.

91. There is one more preliminary paragraph which I must add, with the same view, although in doing so I may incur the risk of its being considered both a digression and egotistical. One of the most important of the five acts of the drama was the great

H

charges by the whole of the French heavy cavalry between La Haye Sainte and Hougoumont, in order to gain the battle promptly by breaking and destroying the centre of the Anglo-Allied line of battle. Now the reader cannot understand the narrative of this great incident of the battle, without a knowledge of how it was foreseen that such an attack was probable at some period of the action; how it arose that preparation was made for meeting it; and what the formation of the 3rd division actually was by which it was met and resisted: the attack having chiefly fallen on that division.

92. When, on the morning of the 18th of June, the enemy's formation clearly indicated an attack on the British position, General the Prince of Orange, who commanded the corps, and General Baron Alten, who commanded the third division, discussed for some time how the division should be formed in order of battle. The Duke of Wellington, having joined them during the discussion, and being referred to, replied shortly, " Form in the usual way ;" and rode on. This did not solve the difficulty, as it was felt that the position of the division exposed it greatly to the fire of the enemy's artillery, and to the action of his numerous and formidable cavalry. The discussion having been continued for some time after the Duke had gone, and no determination arrived at, I asked General Alten if he would allow me to form the

division; to this he at once and unqualifiedly assented; upon which I instantly left him, and proceeded with the formation. In order to understand the formation it is necessary to examine the accompanying Sketch, made by me on the morning of the 19th of June, 1815: the following is an explana-

FORMATION OF THE THIRD DIVISION AT WATERLOO.

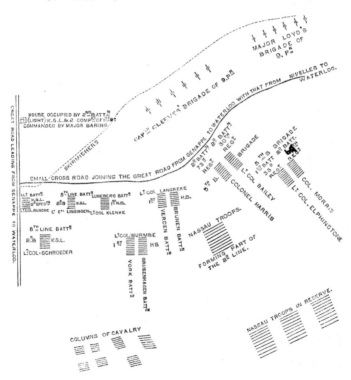

The left of the division rested on the road leading from Genappe to Mont St. Jean, on which the 5th division had its right. The right extended to the 1st division. A company of field yagers were detached to the wood occupied by the 1st division.

Fifth British brigade, Sir Colin Halkett.

Second K. G. L. brigade, Colonel Ompteda.

First Hanoverian ditto, Count Kielmansegge.

tion of that sketch :—The 3rd division was composed of
three brigades, as shown by the sketch ; its numerical
strength was about 6000 men.   The principles and
considerations which guided me in making the formation were as follow :—The French cavalry had, on
the 16th, proved itself very formidable at Quatre
Bras in its attacks upon the third division.   That
cavalry, in immensely augmented numbers, was now
forming opposite to the division, and the ground
between them and us presented no natural obstacle
whatever.   It was at the same time evident, from
the way in which the French guns were taking up
their ground, that the division would be exposed to a
severe artillery fire.   It was, therefore, of the highest
importance that the formation of the division should
be such that its passing from line into a formation
for resisting cavalry should be as rapid as possible ;
and that the re-formation of the line should also be
made rapidly.   To carry these views into effect the
strong battalions formed each an oblong on the two
centre companies, and, when the battalions were weak,
two were joined, the right-hand battalion of the two
forming left in front, and the left-hand battalion
right in front, each in column of companies.   The
fronts of the oblongs were formed by four companies ;
the rear faces of the oblongs were of the same strength ;
and the sides of one company each, which were formed
by the outward wheel of subdivisions.   It will be

observed that, when a battalion forms oblong in this manner upon the two centre companies, the formation is made in *less* than half the time in which it would form square on a flank company; and the same applies to the deployment. Thus, supposing a battalion of 10 companies, the formation of oblong on the two centre companies, or the deployment from the two centre companies, requires only the time for the march of the length occupied by the front of four companies; while, from the formation on a flank company, the formation of a square, or a deployment, requires the time necessary to march the length occupied by the front of nine companies; that is, the time required is *more* than double.

93. As will be seen by the sketch, the front line consisted of five of these oblongs, and the second line of four of them; and they were so placed as to be as nearly as possible in exchequer; that is, placed in such a way that the oblongs of the second line stood opposite to the openings of the first line, as shown on the sketch.

94. It will be observed by the sketch that one battalion of the Nassau troops formed part of the second line of the order of battle of the third division, and that three others stood as a reserve to the division. This arose from an accidental circumstance. On forming the division, I found that there were not troops enough to complete the second line, and, seeing

the Nassau troops near at hand, and not in the order
of battle, I proposed to General Kruse to adopt the
formation as shown on the sketch ; but saying to him
at the same time, that I had not the slightest authority for asking him to do so.   With a frankness that
showed the true spirit of the man, he at once said
that he approved and would adopt the formation ;
and I of course, as soon as possible, asked General
Alten's sanction, who approved.   These arrangements were only in preparation ; the division remained deployed in two lines, its proper order of
battle, but ready to form in oblongs when such formation might be required : while merely under the
continued severe cannonade, the division lay down in
line.

95. *Commencement of the Action.*—The first firing
that took place at the battle of Waterloo was at half
past eleven o'clock A.M. ; the first cannon-shot then
fired marked exactly the commencement of this great
contest.   The action was begun by an attack on
Hougoumont by the three divisions, commanded by
Prince Jerome, Foy, and Bachelu, forming the 2nd
corps under Reille.   This attack was unaccompanied
with any other, except that of a general cannonade
on the centre of the Anglo-Allied line.   It was quite,
therefore, an isolated attack.   This attack was begun
by Jerome's division, and supported by the other two
divisions of the corps.   It was made in the usual

style, that is, by a swarm of skirmishers supported
by columns. Siborne is mistaken in saying that
Cleeves's brigade of guns opened upon Jerome's supporting columns; they opened upon a column of
Bachelu's division that was marching diagonally
across the field towards the wood of Hougoumont.
Cleeves could not have fired over the enclosures of
Hougoumont on the columns of Jerome's division;
this is one of the very few errors of detail to be found
in Siborne's wonderfully accurate work. The fire
from Cleeves's battery was very effective; it caused
the column against which it was directed to swerve
off to its left, and altogether from the point to which
it was directed.

96. The French skirmishers and their supports,
advancing in their usual dashing style, gained possession of most of the wood; but the Nassau battalion
and Hanoverian riflemen, who defended it, being supported by the fire of Bull's guns, and by a spirited
advance of the light companies of the Guards, the
French were driven from it.

97. The cannonade was now become general and
severe upon the whole centre of the Anglo-Allied
line. Jerome renewed, with increased vigour, his
attack upon Hougoumont, in which he was supported
by Foy's division, and after a most severe struggle
they gained the wood; but they were brought to a
complete stand when they advanced upon the south

wall of the garden, from which they received a severe fire, and were driven back. That wall was concealed from them by the small orchard on its south, and, being driven back from the wall, they had to find shelter in the wood. Two of Boult's guns under Major Napier, Smith's brigade of guns, and Major Sympher's brigade of guns, were all brought to bear on the defence of the Hougoumont enclosures during this renewed attack.

98. The French were again driven back from the occupation of that part of the wood nearest to the garden; but being strongly reinforced, they not only regained it, but pushed on in such force as to drive back the light companies of the Coldstream and 3rd Guards, who retired into the farmyard by the gateway that fronted to the Allied position, and, shutting that gateway, used all the means at hand by which to barricade it : the French forced an entrance, but the intruders were shot down. A most gallant hand-to-hand struggle ended in the repulse of the assailants, and they never afterwards succeeded in getting into any part of the buildings; nor did they ever succeed in possessing themselves of any part of the garden. At the same time that they failed in forcing their way into the buildings, they crossed the avenue which led from the buildings to the Nivelles road; but from this advanced position they were driven back by four companies of the Coldstream

## PLAN OF HOUGOUMONT.

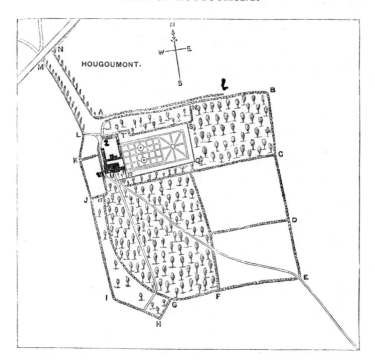

A. B. C. D. E. F. G. J. Farm of Hougoumont, surrounded by hedge and ditch.

F. G. J. Wood masking the enclosure from the French.

T. U. Farm-court and building.

U. Double gates leading into court-yard, forced by the French but never held.

Q. R. S. T. Walled enclosure of the garden, loopholed by the British troops.

Guards, under Colonel Woodford; part of these four companies reinforced the garrison of the buildings, entering by the door in the lane, and part occupied the enclosures along the avenue.

99. The failure of the attacks upon the buildings and garden led the French to attack the orchard, which was vigorously defended by Lord Saltoun with the light companies of the 1st brigade of Guards, who ultimately retired to, and maintained himself, behind the northern enclosure of the great orchard; when, reinforced by two companies of the 3rd Guards, he advanced, and, driving the French from the orchard, occupied its southern enclosure, which is in a line with the southern garden-wall.

100. The second act of the great drama commenced at half-past one o'clock P.M. No one can doubt, who knows the field of battle, and who is even tolerably informed of the circumstances, that Napoleon's plan of attack was that of breaking Wellington's centre at La Haye Sainte, overthrowing the left of the Allied line, and thus going far to ensure the defeat of the Anglo-Allied army; to separate it entirely from that of Blucher; and to gain the command of the great road to Brussels. Two hours had been lost to Napoleon in the attack of Hougoumont, which attack was only an auxiliary operation to the main one by which he hoped to gain the battle. During these two hours Ney was preparing for making the intended great

attack on the centre and left of the Anglo-Allied line.
For this purpose he placed in position, on the central
rise of ground that was between the main ridges on
which the armies stood, a battery of 74 pieces of
artillery, so that its fire might bear directly upon
the right of Picton's, and on the left of Alten's divisions, and upon La Haye Sainte. (See Sketch, p. 94,
and paragraphs 79 and 80.) The right of Picton's
division was on the left of the Charleroi road, the left
of Alten's was on that road, and La Haye Sainte was
upon it : this was the very centre of the Allied army,
so that breaking in upon and gaining this part of the
position was the all-important object which Napoleon
had in view.

101. The battery of 74 guns, of which part were
12-pounders, was at the distance of only 250 yards
from La Haye Sainte, and about 600 yards from the
Anglo-Allied position : it both covered the French
troops in their advance to attack, and caused great
loss in the Anglo-Allied line. This great attack on
the Allied centre was made by the advance in columns
of the whole of D'Erlon's corps; Bachelu's division
of Reille's corps was placed in support of it on the
lower, that is the intermediate ridge, the position of
this division being opposite to La Haye Sainte on
the west of the Charleroi road.

102. The whole of D'Erlon's four divisions advanced to the attack, in imposing masses, about half-

past one o'clock, thickly covering their whole front
with skirmishers; the actual collision commenced a
little before two o'clock.   The left attack was made
by Donzelot's division, one brigade of which marched
upon the enclosures of La Haye Sainte, and the other
against Kempt's brigade.   On Donzelot's right was
the division of Alix, and on Alix's right was the
division of Marcognet—these two divisions forming
the centre of the attacking force ; while Durutte's
division formed the right of the attack, being opposite to Papelotte, La Haye, and Smohain.

103. The brigade of Donzelot's division which
attacked the enclosures of La Haye Sainte was supported by a large body of heavy cavalry, and succeeded in gaining possession of both the orchard and
garden, and in repulsing, with great loss, a battalion
of Ompteda's brigade, that was advanced to assist in
the defence of the enclosures : the companies of Major
Baring's battalion that attempted the defence of the
orchard and garden were obliged to enter the buildings.   Thus the French got possession of the orchard
and garden, but not of any of the buildings, the garrison of which was increased by some of the skirmishers
who had been advanced to assist in the defence of the
enclosures, and found shelter in the buildings.

Simultaneously with this attack upon La Haye
Sainte, the attacks upon Kempt's and Pack's brigades,
and on the left of the allied line, were in progress.

Donzelot's right brigade and Alix's division, supported on its right by Marcognet's division, advanced in heavy columns, and attacked Kempt's and Pack's brigades. The column of attack on Kempt's brigade seemed to be checked by the fire of artillery, and by the musketry fire from the troops lining the hedge, and showed hesitation when about a hundred yards from the hedge, to gain which was the real object of their attack. This hesitation was taken advantage of, and an advance of the right of Kempt's brigade was completely successful in causing the retreat of the brigade of Donzelot that was opposed to it. But the division of Alix, advancing boldly into the opening between Kempt's and Pack's brigades, turned Kempt's right, upon which the left wing of the 28th Regiment formed to its left, thus separating from the right wing. This brought its fire to bear upon Alix's division, and protected Kempt's left. Alix was now passing through the opening between Kempt's and Pack's brigade; Marcognet was in severe conflict with Pack's brigade; Durutte had got possession of Papelotte; Kempt had defeated the troops in his front; the wood and garden of La Haye Sainte were in the hands of the French; and a strong body of French cavalry, after nearly destroying a Hanoverian battalion, was advancing beyond the enclosures of La Haye Sainte. It was at this moment,

and under these circumstances, that Lord Anglesea
ordered Lord Edward Somerset's and General Ponsonby's brigades of cavalry to charge ; Somerset's,
with Anglesea himself at their head, on the right
and Ponsonby on the left of the Charleroi road.
Somerset's brigade, meeting the French heavy
cavalry on the slope from the Allied position,
defeated the French cuirassiers in the most brilliant
manner ; and crossing the road, assisted Kempt's
brigade in clearing their front. I believe this to
have been the only fairly tested fight of cavalry
against cavalry during the day. It was a fair
meeting of two bodies of heavy cavalry, each in
perfect order. The subsequent attacks were either
those of heavy cavalry against heavy cavalry that
had been previously wrecked upon squares of
infantry, or contests between light and heavy
cavalry.

104. The attack by Ponsonby's brigade was
most brilliant and most successful. The two regiments which formed the right of his brigade, the
Royals and the Inniskillens, defeated Alix's division ; and the Greys, passing through Pack's
brigade, defeated the part of Marcognet's division
which was in conflict with that brigade. The
three regiments of Ponsonby's brigade, continuing
their impetuous advance across the Wavre road,
and through the hedge, completed the defeat of all

the columns of French infantry that were engaged
in the attack on Picton's division.  The French loss
was very great in killed, wounded, and prisoners.
The noble impetuosity of Ponsonby's magnificent
brigade impelled it to a further advance, in which
it charged and threw into the utmost disorder
the great French battery, and caused it considerable
loss; but this exposed the brigade to suffer very
severely from the fire of the French batteries and
reserves, and to be attacked by Jaquinot's division
and part of Milhaud's cuirassiers.  From these
attacks it suffered great loss, and was not able
to secure all its prisoners.

The farm of Papelotte was retaken by the
troops under Prince Bernhard of Saxe-Weimar; so
that this great attack on the centre and left of the
Anglo-Allied army had no result favourable to
the French Emperor; he had not gained anything
in advance by the attack; even the enclosures of
La Haye Sainte were not retained.  Much time
had been lost, and a great sacrifice of men had
been made; certainly more than that suffered by
the Anglo-Allied army.  One alarming circumstance
for the Anglo-Allied army had occurred during this
attack, the retreat of Bylandt's Dutch-Belgian
brigade, which, leaving its position on the first
advance of the French attacking columns, retreated
through the British line, and placed itself on the

reverse slope of the position, against orders and
remonstrances, and took no further part in the
action!

105. Sir John Lambert's brigade, which, until
the advance of Ponsonby's brigade, had been kept
in reserve near to the farm of Mont St. Jean,
advanced and took up its position on the right of
Kempt's brigade, with its right on the Charleroi
road. This movement of Lambert's brigade, together with Pack's brigade having closed to Kempt's
left, filled up that opening of the Anglo-Allied line
which was caused by the retreat of Bylandt's
brigade. From the time that Kempt's brigade
advanced through the hedge in its front, and across
the Wavre road, the command of the division
devolved upon him, Picton having fallen at that
time. (See Map at the end.) At the same time
that Lambert's, Kempt's, and Pack's brigades took
up their altered position, and that Kempt's riflemen
re-occupied the knoll in their front, the garrison of
La Haye Sainte was reinforced by two companies,
and now, therefore, consisted of six companies.

106. Napoleon intrusted to Ney the general
arrangement of this great attack on the Allied centre
and left. Immediately before authorizing Ney to
begin the attack, Napoleon saw a portion of the
Prussian advance guard in the direction of the wood
of Paris, and in consequence ordered the cavalry

divisions of Daumont and Subervie to leave their
position in the order of battle and to meet this
attack. Napoleon now knew positively, from the
report of a Prussian officer who had been made
prisoner, that the troops seen in the direction of
the wood of Paris were Prussians. These two
divisions of French cavalry were afterwards supported by the infantry divisions of Simner and
Jeannin, which prevented the employment of any
part of that force, at any period of the action,
against Wellington's line of battle.

107. It will be observed that, during this great
attack upon the left centre and left of Wellington's
line of battle, the whole of the right centre and
right was free from attack, with the exception of
a cannonade; during which time the troops lay
down on the interior slope of the position, and were
thus partly sheltered by the ground. The attack
on Hougoumont was continued, but not in such
a manner as to give any apprehension of its being
taken. This great attack, therefore, upon Wellington's centre and left, had the serious defect to the
attacking force of being only a partial one : its
result to the French army was that of having lost
a great many more in killed, wounded, and prisoners than had been lost by the Allies; of having
had a large portion of the infantry thrown into
considerable confusion; of having had from 30 to

I

40 guns injured; and of having lost three hours without effecting anything whatever against the Anglo-Allied position.

108. The interval between this attack and the next was very considerable, and no one in the Anglo-Allied line could imagine what the next move would be;—that is, how the third act of the drama would begin; and when it did open, it was certainly in a manner quite unexpected. General Alten and his staff, being near to where the Belgian Lion now stands, had a commanding view of the enemy's position and movements, and watched with anxiety during this lull of the action what the next move of the French would be. The attacks on La Haye Sainte and Hougoumont were continued, but not with much violence, and the cannonade was moderate. But at about four o'clock the cannonade became violent in the extreme, probably as much so as has been witnessed in any open field of battle. This was evidently the prelude to some serious attack. To our surprise we soon saw that it was the prelude to an attack of cavalry upon a grand scale. Such an attack we had fully anticipated (see paragraphs 9 and 10) would take place at some period of the day; but we had no idea that it would be made upon our line standing in its regular order of battle, and that line as yet unshaken by any previous attack by infantry. The

moment that it was observed that the movement
of the great masses of the French heavy cavalry
were directed towards his division, General Alten
passed the order to form oblongs, into which formation the division rapidly passed; the Guards
formed squares on the right of the 3rd division; the
two divisions thus filling up the space between
the Charleroi and Nivelles roads; the artillery stood
in front of the infantry on the front slope of the
position, so that its fire might be effectual against
the attacking force.  (For this position of the 3rd
division see Sketch, p. 99, taken by me on the ground
on the morning of the 19th.)

109. The French force which we saw advancing
to the attack was the whole of Milhaud's corps, consisting of forty squadrons of heavy cavalry.  That
corps, being on the French right of the Charleroi
road, had to cross the road before making this attack,
and had consequently to oblique considerably to its
left.  This was effected in beautiful order, and the
formation and advance of that magnificent and highly
disciplined cavalry had, as a spectacle, a very grand
effect.  These splendid horsemen were enthusiastic
in the cause of Napoleon—full of confidence in him
and in themselves—thirsting to revenge the reverses
which had been suffered by the French armies—led
by most experienced and able cavalry commanders—
and they submitted to a rigid discipline.  Their

advance to the attack was splendid and interesting in the extreme. Our surprise at being so soon attacked by this great and magnificent force of cavalry was accompanied with the opinion that the attack was premature, and that we were perfectly prepared and secure against its effects, so far as any military operation can be calculated upon.

110. This grand attack of cavalry was made in lines of columns : these lines filled much of the space between the enclosures of La Haye Sainte and Hougoumont, from each of which they of course kept at some distance to avoid the infantry fire from them. The guns of Cleeves and Lloyd were taken at the first onset of these horsemen ; but their fire, which was admirably directed, had been highly destructive ; the men and officers of these two brigades took shelter within the oblongs. The French cavalry advanced upon the oblongs, the fire from the front faces of which was given at about thirty yards' distance. This caused the attacking cavalry to swerve to the right and left of the front faces of the squares, as usually has been the case in attacks of cavalry against infantry ; but although they did not gallop in mass right on the bayonets of the infantry, they made every other effort to enter the oblongs, by firing into them, cutting aside the bayonets, and surrounding the oblongs to obtain a point of entrance. Those who were not immediately opposite to the faces of the

oblongs passed the first and attacked the oblongs of
the second line, showing great gallantry and persevering obstinacy to win; but all their efforts failed,
and they had received the artillery fire, and were
exposed to the fire of the front, flank, and rear faces
of the oblongs: thus their numbers became fearfully
diminished, and this splendid body of cavalry became
a wreck, surrounded by the immovable masses of
infantry within the formations of which it had become
entangled. While in this hopeless condition, it was
driven down the exterior slope by the Anglo-Allied
cavalry.

111. Soon, however, recovering their formation,
the same forty squadrons resumed the charge, keeping
a reserve in hand; and after further similar gallant
but unsuccessful efforts against the oblongs, they were
again, when in a state of utter confusion, driven
down the exterior slope of the position by the Anglo-
Allied cavalry.

112. Napoleon, having witnessed the defeat of his
cavalry, ordered that Milhaud should renew the attack,
and that Kellermann's corps should join in it: whether
Napoleon ordered or allowed Guyot to join in the
attack, is doubtful; but, whether by Napoleon's wish
or not, Guyot did join in the attack with the cavalry
of the Guard. This third attack of cavalry consisted
of 77 squadrons, and was one of the most powerful
efforts ever made by cavalry against infantry in the

history of war.   When it is considered that about
12,000 men were employed in this attack, and that
only 1000 horsemen could stand in line on the 1000
yards which separate the enclosures of La Haye
Sainte and Hougoumont—that, therefore, twelve different ranks, two deep, could assail in succession the
Allied force opposed to it—and when, further, the
composition of this force is considered, and the reputation of its leaders, its imposing character becomes
evident.   It will be recollected that these horsemen
could advance on a front of only 500 yards, as they
were obliged to keep at some distance from the
enclosures of both Hougoumont and La Haye Sainte ;
and it will also be recollected that the fire of artillery,
under the protection of which this vast force of
cavalry advanced to make its attacks, was of the most
formidable character.

113. Nearly the whole of the ground between La
Haye Sainte and Hougoumont was covered with this
splendid array of horsemen : their advance to the
attack, made in a manner that showed the highest
discipline, was majestic and imposing.   The attacks
upon the oblongs were made with much enthusiasm
and obstinacy ; but in no instance was there one of
them penetrated or overthrown, although several of
them were formed by very young and totally inexpe-
rienced troops.   These 77 magnificent squadrons, after
using their best endeavours to overthrow the infantry,

suffered such severe loss by the fire of artillery and infantry as to be thrown into hopeless confusion, and were driven by the Allied cavalry down the exterior slope of the position.

114. They soon rallied, and renewed the attack with the same daring spirit as before, but with the same results; for they were again thrown into a state of hopeless confusion by the enormous loss they suffered under the fire of the squares and oblongs, and in this state were again driven down the exterior slope by the cavalry at about half-past five o'clock; this third great act of the drama having continued about two hours, that is, from four till six o'clock.

115. The results to Napoleon of these four grand cavalry attacks were, that he had lost two hours, and suffered such enormous loss of his heavy cavalry as to render it inefficient for any great effort during the further course of the battle. This most serious loss of time, and enormous and irreparable loss of cavalry, were uncompensated for by his having obtained any advantage whatever.

To understand these great cavalry attacks, it is necessary to bear in mind the extraordinary fact that the large bodies of Dutch-Belgian cavalry, and the regiment of Cumberland Hussars, that stood in reserve behind the 1st and 3rd divisions of infantry, took no part in the action; the only cavalry which did act being the small remains of Lord Edward Somerset's brigade, the 3rd Hussars of the King's German Legion, and part of Grant's brigade. Just before the first advance of Milhaud to the attack, about four o'clock, Piré moved to his left, threatening the Allied right, which was met by a corresponding move of Grant's brigade to his right; but seeing that Piré's movement was only to draw attention from the real attack, Grant returned with five squadrons of his brigade, and shared in resisting the great attacks.

116. To understand this third act of the great drama, and how the battle stood during it—that is, during and at the termination of these grand cavalry attacks on the centre of Wellington's line—it is necessary to advert to the progress made by the Prussians. About half-past four o'clock a part of Bulow's corps debouched from the wood of Paris, and the 6th French corps under Lobau, and the cavalry divisions of Daumont and Subervie, opposed them. Blucher sent some troops to secure the possession of Frischermont and Smohain. By six o'clock Blucher had 29,000 men and 64 guns in presence against Napoleon's right: their position, when deployed, was parallel to the Charleroi road; they were now getting seriously engaged with the French reserves, and assumed a highly formidable attitude, not only threatening the defeat of Napoleon's right wing, but also appearing likely to gain the Charleroi road in rear of the French army.

117. The general result of the action at the conclusion of this the third great attack—that is, at six
o'clock P.M.—was, that the heavy cavalry on both
sides was so much exhausted as to be unfit for any
great effort during the remaining part of the action ;
that the loss of infantry on the part of the French
army was greater than that of the Allied army ; that
Napoleon had not, in the six hours and a half during
which his attacks had continued, gained any advantage
whatever over the Anglo-Allied army ; and the loss
of so much time had enabled the Prussians firmly to
establish a formidable force for the attack of his right,
and threatening his rear. This state of things obliged
Napoleon, at this period of the battle, to employ 12
battalions of the infantry of the Guard to oppose the
Prussian attack : the whole of the infantry of the
Guard was composed of 24 battalions. The French
army was now so overmatched numerically as to be
called upon to display, and it did display, great
discipline and great enthusiasm in the cause of its
leader, and made the most devoted sacrifices to win
the day.

118. It must have become evident to Napoleon,
considerably before its final repulse, that the cavalry
attack on the Allied centre was a failure. He in consequence arranged a renewed attack of infantry,
immediately previous to the final repulse of his cavalry,
with the view of getting possession of La Haye Sainte,

and thus breaking through the centre of the Allied
line.

*Fourth great Attack.*—This was the fourth great
attack. It was intrusted to Ney, who, on receiving
an order to carry it into execution, asked to be reinforced—a request that Napoleon had not the means
of complying with. Ney then proceeded to carry the
order into execution with the force at his disposal,
and the first great effort was made against La Haye
Sainte. The assailants attacked it with the greatest
fury, and after a desperate fight carried it about the
same time that the last of the great cavalry attacks
was repulsed, that is, about six o'clock P.M. The
original garrison of La Haye Sainte, it will be recollected, consisted of the 2nd light battalion of the
King's German Legion, numbering 400 men, and
commanded by Major Baring. The garrison was reinforced in the course of the action by two companies
of the 1st light battalion of the King's German
Legion, after the repulse of the first great attack on
Wellington's centre and left; about four o'clock by
the light company of the 5th line battalion of the
King's German Legion; and subsequently by two
flank companies of the 1st Regiment of Nassau;
making in all reinforcements of five companies.
Much has been said of Baring's having sent repeatedly
for ammunition, and that none was sent to him.
This matter had certainly been grossly mismanaged.

The arrangement for the brigades getting their spare ammunition was, that each brigade should communicate with the guard over the ammunition, and order forward what was wanted. How the brigade failed to do this has not been explained, as so many of its superior officers fell in the action. Baring could not account for it, which I know from our having slept together on the ground close to the Wellington Tree on the night after the action, when he mentioned his having sent more than once for a supply of ammunition and his having received no answer. The unexplained want of ammunition by Baring's battalion is placed in an extraordinary view when it is considered that the battle of Waterloo lasted eight hours and a half, and that all the three brigades of the division got the ammunition they required, with the exception of this one battalion. The simple fact of Baring's applications for spare ammunition having been made by him late in the day, when, owing to the enemy's position, there could be no certainty of its being got into the place, proves an extraordinary oversight. The spare ammunition should have been sent for early in the morning. What were 60 rounds per man for the defence of such a post? During this attack upon La Haye Sainte, Hougoumont was also seriously attacked; but all the efforts of the French to take it were defeated.

119. The possession of La Haye Sainte by the

French was a very dangerous incident.   It uncovered
the very centre of the Anglo-Allied army, and established the enemy within 60 yards of that centre.
The French lost no time in taking advantage of this,
by pushing forward infantry supported by guns,
which enabled them to maintain a most destructive
fire upon Alten's left and Kempt's right, and to
drive off Kempt's light troops that occupied the knoll
in his front.   By this fire they wasted most seriously
the ranks of the left of Alten's and the right of
Kempt's divisions; so much so that Ompteda's brigade
having been previously nearly destroyed, and Kielmansegge's much weakened, they were now not
sufficiently strong to occupy the front which was
originally assigned to them.   During the progress of
this most severe and very close attack by the French
from La Haye Sainte upon the Anglo-Allied troops
immediately in rear of that farm and its enclosures,
very severe partial attacks were made by infantry,
supported often by cavalry, upon the whole of the
Anglo-Allied troops that occupied the ground between
the Charleroi road and the Nivelles road; and on
the troops which occupied the ground between the
Guards and the Hougoumont enclosures.

120. While these partial but very severe attacks
of cavalry and infantry were carried on in succession
to the great cavalry attacks,—that is, during this
fourth act of the drama,—Du Plat's infantry brigade

of the King's German Legion advanced across the
Nivelles road and took up a position near to the N.E.
angle of the Hougoumont enclosure, where it got into
immediate contact with both cavalry and infantry of
the enemy, and its leader fell. Halkett's Hanoverian
brigade was also advanced across the Nivelles road,
and formed in second line in support of Du Plat's
brigade. Adam's brigade, which, when the action
commenced, stood near to Merbe-Braine, was, early
in the action, moved forward to, and formed on, the
right of the Nivelles road. It was moved across
the Nivelles road about the same time as Du Plat's
brigade, and nearer to the right of the Guards; and
was placed in the hollow which extended from near
the right of the Guards to the Hougoumont enclosure.
The brigade cleared from its front large numbers of
the enemy's skirmishers, and was exposed in that
position to a considerable cannonade, and partial
attacks of cavalry, which caused it to form sometimes
in squares and sometimes in a four-deep formation.
The 52nd was at one time in squares of wings, and
afterwards, the companies having formed their left
behind their right subdivisions, the battalion, by
closing the companies, formed a line four deep, and
continued in that four-deep formation during the remainder of the action. The brigade, being too much
exposed to the cannonade, was withdrawn from its
advanced position in the low ground, to the reverse

slope of the main position, on the right of the Guards;
and there remained until called upon to advance to
meet the advance of the enemy's Imperial Guard,
when, as presently will appear, its services became
eminently important.

121. Wellington, seeing the direction in which the
great cavalry attacks were made, and finding that
no serious attack was made on his right beyond the
Nivelles road, caused Chassé to march from Braine la
Leud with the whole of the Dutch-Belgian division
under his command: it proceeded through Merbe-
Braine to form on the right of the Nivelles road in
rear of the position taken up by Du Plat and Halkett.
This abandonment of the occupation of Braine la
Leud, and thus strengthening his right, and right
centre, by these new dispositions of Du Plat's, Halkett's,
and Chassé's troops, was most judicious on the part
of Wellington; who was eminent, on this great day of
trial, for coolness, judgment, and energy, in doing
everything that the urgencies of the action required
at the proper time; he was never, from the seeming
exigencies of the moment, hurried into an over exertion in support of any particular part of his line of
battle; he managed his reserves in a steady, yet
energetic and masterly manner.

122. It was at this stage of the action that these
great qualities of the Duke were chiefly required and
most fully displayed. We have already seen that La

Haye Sainte was in the hands of the enemy; also the knoll on the opposite side of the road; also the garden and ground on the Anglo-Allied side of it;—that Ompteda's brigade was nearly annihilated, and Kielmansegge's so thinned, that those two brigades could not hold their position. That part of the field of battle, therefore, which was between Halkett's left and Kempt's right, was unprotected; and being the very centre of the Duke's line of battle, was consequently that point, above all others, which the enemy wished to gain. The danger was imminent; and at no other period of the action was the result so precarious as at this moment. Most fortunately Napoleon did not support the advantage his troops had gained at this point, by bringing forward his reserve; proving that he did not exert that activity and personal energy, in superintending and conforming to the progress of the action, which he ought to have done.

123. The Duke of Wellington stood at this moment on the left of the Nivelles road, behind the left of Maitland's brigade of Guards. The Prince of Orange, Count Alten, and so many officers of the 3rd division, had, before this event happened, been killed, or wounded and obliged to leave the field, that I did not then know, nor do I now know, who was, at the moment I allude to, senior officer of the division on the field: I therefore, as the staff-officer present, galloped

direct to the Duke, and informed him that his line
was open for the whole space between Halkett's and
Kempt's brigades.   This very startling information
he received with a degree of coolness, and replied to
in an instant with such precision and energy, as to
prove the most complete self-possession ; and left on
my mind the impressions that his Grace's mind remained perfectly calm during every phase, however
serious, of the action ; that he felt confident of his
own powers of being able to guide the storm which
raged around him ; and from the determined manner
in which he then spoke, it was evident that he had
resolved to defend to the last extremity every inch of
the position which he then held.   His Grace's answer
to my representation was in the following words, or
very nearly so :—" I shall order the Brunswick troops
" to the spot, and other troops besides ; go you and
" get all the German troops of the division to the
" spot that you can, and all the guns that you can
" find."

124. Of such gravity did Wellington consider this
great gap in the very centre of his line of battle, that
he not only ordered the Brunswick troops there, but
put himself at their head ; and it was even then with
the greatest difficulty that the ground could be held ;
but Count Kielmansegge soon led back his gallant
Germans to the spot ; the Brunswickers held their
ground supported by part of the Nassau force ; and

ultimately Vivian's brigade of cavalry supported these troops; and the artillery officers responded to the utmost of their available means in strengthening this most vulnerable and dangerous part of the position.

In no other part of the action was the Duke of Wellington exposed to so much personal risk as on this occasion, as he was necessarily under a close and most destructive infantry fire at a very short distance; at no other period of the day were his great qualities as a commander so strongly brought out, for it was the moment of his greatest peril as to the result of the action. This peril was undoubtedly in a great measure the fruit of the vast importance of holding La Haye Sainte not having been seen, and the consequent neglect of its defences; but the error was most ably and nobly amended. The troops that gallantly and successfully secured this part of the position for the rest of the day, could not have been expected to make the stand which they did against such determined and protracted efforts of veteran French troops; they were only recent formations, and without experience in the field.

125. It is necessary to consider how the action stood at the termination of this the fourth great attack on the Allied line of battle; that is to say, at half-past seven o'clock. The fourth attack had not, like the three previous ones, been without success

K

on the part of the assailants.  They had gained La
Haye Sainte and its enclosures; held advantageous
ground on its right and front; and were thus most
advantageously placed for breaking through  the
Allied centre by a powerful effort of their  reserves
upon that point, supported by a general attack upon
the whole line : but fortunately for the Allies, Napoleon did not seem to watch the progress of the action
so closely as to act promptly in conformity with its
changes.   He failed to take advantage of the  success
which he had gained by the advance of his troops
from La Haye Sainte when that part of the Anglo-
Allied line was nearly denuded of troops : and when
he did ultimately strike for victory by the advance of
his reserve, that is of the Imperial Guard, he gave it
a wrong direction, as will soon appear ; for it is clear
that the Guard would have had much more chance of
success in attacking from La Haye Sainte than from
any other point ; its advance would have been covered
to within 60 yards of the Anglo-Allied line ; its left
by Reille's corps ; its right by that of D'Erlon.

126. At this time, say half-past seven o'clock, the
Prussian attack on Napoleon's right had become much
more serious.  It is necessary therefore, in order to
understand fully the progress of the action up to this
period, that a retrospect should be taken of the whole
operation of the Prussian army in its movement to
support Wellington at Waterloo.  On the 17th of

June Wellington informed Blucher of his falling back to the position of Waterloo, and he knew that Blucher had fallen back to Wavre. The Duke informed Blucher that he would accept battle in the position of Waterloo, if Blucher would support him with two corps of his army. To this proposal Blucher assented, and further said that he would support the Duke with his whole army.

In order at all to understand the views of the Duke of Wellington as to accepting battle on the field of Waterloo, it is essential to keep this arrangement fully in view; otherwise the Duke might justly be accused of the utmost temerity and folly in accepting battle, as much the greater portion of his army (see paragraph 12) consisted of mere Landwehr, and of Dutch-Belgian troops. The latter, from political and other causes, could not be depended upon; which, in fact, had been already proved on the 16th. It would be an error to suppose that it was from any want of courage that the Dutch-Belgian troops could not be depended upon : proof enough exists that the people of those countries are capable of the most heroic and persevering exertions when engaged in a cause that they care to support; but under the circumstances in which they were placed on this occasion, they were without confidence, were not acting in a cause which they cordially supported, and showed that it was not

one in which they wished to oppose themselves
seriously to French troops.

127. In order to see what means there were of
carrying into effect the arrangements made by
Blucher and Wellington, that the Prussian army
should support Wellington on the field of Waterloo,
it is necessary to consider the position of Blucher's
army, that of his opponent Grouchy, the distances
each had to march, the state of the roads, and the
marches which each actually accomplished.

128. Napoleon on the 17th of June placed about
32,000 men (among whom were 45 squadrons of
cavalry) under the orders of Grouchy, to follow the
Prussian army, which had on the previous day lost
the battle of Ligny. This force, having been detached
late on the 17th, only got to Gembloux late in the
evening, and marched between seven and eight o'clock
next morning in the direction of Wavre; near to which
place Blucher had assembled the whole of his force,
including Bülow's corps, on the evening of the 17th.
The distance from Gembloux to Wavre is 12 miles,
by a road that is almost in a straight line, and better
than the usual cross-roads. The distance from
Wavre to the centre of Wellington's position behind
La Haye Sainte is 10 miles; the distance from
Gembloux to the centre of Wellington's position
behind La Haye Sainte is 20 miles; the distance

from Wavre to St. Lambert is 5 miles; the distance
from Mont St. Guibert to St. Lambert, by the bridge
over the Dyle at Moustier, is 7 miles. Such are the
distances as shown by the map of Ferrari, and by the
great topographical map since published at Brussels.
But although it is necessary to know the distances, it
is not less necessary to know that the cross-roads on
which Grouchy and Blucher operated were at that
time so wet and soft as to be all but impassable. In
fact, whenever the troops left the great chaussées they
were placed in situations of great difficulty. This
was proved on the 17th of June by the movement of
the 3rd division through Wais le Hutte, where it
crossed the Dyle, and its march was ordered to be
by cross-roads parallel to the great chaussée. After
crossing the Dyle the march on the cross-roads became
so difficult as absolutely to make the situation of the
division in some degree perilous; it did lose some of
its baggage; and the division felt as relieved from a
very unpleasant situation when it moved, without
orders from head-quarters, but by obvious necessity,
into the great chaussée. This will at once show the
vast difficulty that Blucher and Grouchy found in
those cross-roads, and they had no other to march
upon in their movements on the 17th and 18th of
June. It is impossible indeed to understand how
Grouchy could have accomplished, even had he intended to do so, the march of twenty miles from

Gembloux to Mont St. Jean, on the 18th, over such
roads; and perfectly easy, for any one who saw the
3rd division floundering through a few miles of
them, to understand why even the leading brigade of
Bülow's corps, which marched at four o'clock in the
morning on the 18th, was eight hours in marching
between eight and nine miles; although that brigade
met with no obstacle but the badness of the road,
which had not then been at all cut up by the previous
passage of troops.

129. Blucher, in order to fulfil his promise to
Wellington, of supporting him on the field of
Waterloo with his whole army, put Bülow's corps
in motion at four o'clock on the morning of the
18th, which was followed by Pirch's corps. These
two corps marched by St. Lambert on the wood of
Paris; and Zieten's corps, which moved some hours
later, marched by Ohain upon the hamlet of Smohain. Thielemann's corps was to form the reserve,
and to follow the march of the corps of Zieten; but
before his intended movement commenced, he was
attacked by a superior force under Grouchy, who
had moved with his whole force upon Wavre, and
Thielemann was in consequence engaged during the
whole day in resisting that attack. But the other
three corps of the Prussian army continued their
march towards the field of Waterloo. The march
of Bülow's corps, and of Pirch's corps, was delayed

for a considerable time by the extraordinary accident of a fire taking place in the town of Wavre at the moment of their passing through it.   But Bülow's advanced guard had passed through Wavre previously, and was thus in some measure separated from the rest of the corps, and continued its march to the wood of Paris.   This advanced guard of the Prussian army was allowed to take undisputed possession of the wood of Paris, which secured for the corps of Bülow and Pirch a débouchée upon the right flank and rear of the French army.   But although the advanced guard got possession of the wood of Paris by twelve o'clock, it remained concealed in the wood, not being strong enough to advance beyond it.   The 15th and 16th brigades of Bülow's corps followed the advanced guard, and had great difficulty in their march from the badness of the road, and the pass of St. Lambert presented difficulties that seemed insurmountable.   Violent rain, which began about three o'clock on the 17th, continued through the night.   This violent rain fell upon the whole of the country on which the armies of Wellington, Blucher, and Napoleon marched during the 17th, and rendered the cross-roads in the whole of that country all but impassable on the 18th.   In the pass of St. Lambert the carriages sank to their axles, and both men and horses sank so deep in the wet ground as to render it very doubtful whether

the passage could be effected. The high spirit of
Blücher, and his great influence with the troops,
did much to surmount the difficulty. He said that
he had pledged his word to Wellington that he
would support him, and that all difficulties must be
overcome by perseverance, and that he must keep
his promise. The passage of the defile was at last
effected by the 15th and 16th brigades, and they
reached the wood of Paris at four o'clock.

130. It was not Blucher's intention to have débouched from the wood of Paris until Bülow's and
Pirch's corps were up; but he now determined to
do so with even the small force which had reached
it, as he was aware, from the messages which he
had received from Wellington, and from what
he now saw of the field of battle, that the attack
upon the Allied line had become very serious.
With the view, therefore, of relieving Wellington,
so far as was within his power, although at considerable risk to himself, Blucher débouched at
half-past four o'clock P.M. from the wood of Paris,
with the advanced guard, the 15th and 16th brigades
of infantry, the reserve cavalry, and artillery; two
battalions from the 16th brigade marched to the left
of the valley of the Lasne, and three battalions
from the 15th brigade marched to Frischermont
and Smohain. By these very judicious movements,
both flanks of the force débouching from the wood

of Paris were protected, and Blucher only advanced the remainder of the small force with which he was now acting, sufficiently to bring on a cannonade, and to draw upon him the full attention of the enemy. Napoleon, seeing this attack, ordered it to be met by the 6th corps under Lobau, and by Daumont's and Subervie's cavalry; and moved forward the Guard to the high ground behind La Belle Alliance to replace the 6th corps. Blucher, by half-past five o'clock, took up a position extending from Frischermont on the right to the valley of the Lasne on the left. In this position a severe cannonade and some partial attacks took place between the forces under Blucher and Lobau, but without any material result. Blucher was, however, soon joined by the 13th and 14th brigades, and had, therefore, about six o'clock, the whole of Bülow's corps in the position, as above, between Frischermont and the Lasne, opposed to the force under Lobau. The force under Lobau consisted of 16 battalions, 18 squadrons, and 42 guns; that under Blucher of 36 battalions, 35 squadrons, and 64 guns. Blucher, having detached 6 battalions and 8 squadrons to his right to communicate with Wellington's left, and to act from Smohain and Frischermont, advanced with the remainder of his force, directing his left upon, and in rear of, Planchenoit. Lobau, seeing that he was overmatched, retreated towards the Charleroi road, where the shot from the Prussian guns now began to be felt. Planchenoit was not at that time occupied by French troops, and Napoleon, seeing the absolute necessity of preventing its being occupied by the Prussians, ordered Duhesme to march upon it with 8 battalions of the Guard, and 24 guns, from their position on the right of the chaussée close to Rossomme. Simultaneously with those events, that is about six o'clock P.M., Blucher received information that Thielemann was attacked by a superior force at Wavre; and Ney, having orders to renew the attack on La Haye Sainte, requested reinforcements, which request was said to be met by Napoleon with the expression, " Où voulez-vous que j'en prenne? voulez-vous que j'en fasse ? "

131. The 16th brigade of Bülow's corps advanced to the attack of Planchenoit, now occupied by a portion of the Young Guard under Duhesme, and succeeded in gaining the church and churchyard. But Duhesme having concentrated his attack, and threatened the rear of the Prussian attacking force, the Prussians were driven from the village, and obliged to retire, followed by the French cavalry ; but they were re-formed, and prepared another attack upon the village, reinforced by some battalions. Napoleon, seeing the preparations for a

renewed attack upon Planchenoit, and for turning its right, reinforced it by two battalions of the Old Guard under Morand, who arrived in time to meet the second Prussian attack, which failed; and the Prussians were all driven back upon their main position, which they firmly maintained.

132. Blucher only waited the arrival of Pirch's corps to renew the attack on Planchenoit, and to turn it on its left ; and Napoleon, seeing the importance of such an attack, reinforced Planchenoit by a battalion of the Guard under Pelet ; a battalion of the Guard was at the same time sent from Caillou to the wood of Chantelet to cover the right of the French army. By, say, seven o'clock in the evening, the action had assumed a more serious aspect for Napoleon. Blucher was preparing for a renewed attack with· the corps of Bülow and Pirch upon Planchenoit, and the corps of Zieten was advancing from Smohain on the right and in support of the other two corps ; so that Blucher was now coming into action with three corps of infantry, and a powerful force of artillery and cavalry, amounting to 51,944 men and 104 guns.

133. We are now arrived at that period at which commenced the fifth and last grand attack; that is, the fifth and concluding act of the drama on the field of Waterloo; which freed Europe from any great continental war for forty years.

134. Napoleon determined now to strike for victory. For this purpose, say, at half-past seven o'clock P.M., he ordered 12 battalions of the Imperial Guard, and the divisions of Marcognet, Alix, Donzelot, and Bachelu, to advance to the attack of the Anglo-Allied line, while the divisions of Jerome and Foy renewed the attack on Hougoumont; these attacks were to be supported by a powerful artillery and what remained of the cavalry. While these formidable attacks on the Anglo-Allied line were in progress, Durutte's division opposed the advance of Zieten's corps from Smohain and its vicinity; and Lobau, Daumont, and Subervie, together with 12 battalions of the Imperial Guard, opposed Bülow's and Pirch's corps, and the reserve cavalry of the Prussian army, in the attacks which they made upon Planchenoit and to its right and left. Napoleon pointed out the importance of Planchenoit being held firmly, and Pelet successfully resisted a third attempt by the Prussians to take it; nor did they succeed in taking it until after the failure of the last attack on the Anglo-Allied line.

135. This last grand attack on Wellington's line of battle was the only one of the five which was a combined, general attack : it embraced at once the whole of the Anglo-Allied line. The division of Marcognet attacked Best's brigade; Alix's division attacked Lambert's and Kempt's divisions; Donzelot's

division attacked Alten's division; ten battalions
of the Imperial Guard attacked Maitland's brigade
of Guards and Adam's brigade; and Bachelu's
division advanced in support of the ten battalions
of the Imperial Guard; two battalions of the Guard
were held in reserve. The attack from La Haye
Sainte preceded that by the Guard, as that attack
had never ceased from the taking of that farm, and
increased in intensity as the grand general attack
progressed. The violence of the attack on Hougoumont by Reille's corps was increased to the utter-
most, and extended not only through the wood, but
beyond its eastern enclosure. The attack was preceded along the whole line by a furious cannonade;
and the whole front of attack was covered by a
swarm of skirmishers.

136. The ten battalions of the Imperial Guard
were formed into two columns in mass. The right
column consisted of four battalions of Grenadiers and
Chasseurs of the Middle Guard, in column of divisions
in mass; the left column consisted of six battalions,
also in column of divisions in mass. The leading
four of these six battalions were Grenadiers and
Chasseurs of the Middle Guard: the two rear battalions were Chasseurs of the Old Guard, and were
somewhat to the rear of, and a little to the left of, the
four leading battalions.

137. Napoleon, having placed himself in front of

La Belle Alliance, addressed the battalions of the
Guard as they passed him : they saluted him with loud
cheers.   The four right battalions, in one column, in
mass of divisions, advanced by the tongue of high
ground which extends towards La Belle Alliance,
from where the Belgian Lion now stands ; and the six
battalions on the left advanced very considerably
nearer to the Hougoumont enclosure, its advance being
partly in the lower ground which is on the east of the
great orchard of Hougoumont, from which it swerved
to its right, and gained, and advanced by, the same
tongue of higher ground as that by which the four
battalions had advanced ; but keeping nearer to the
western edge of that tongue of higher ground.
These two columns of attack of the French Imperial
Guard did not attack simultaneously, the attack by
the right column having considerably preceded that
made by the left column.   The head of the right
column directed its march upon that part of the
British position occupied by Maitland's brigade of
Guards, who were lying down, rather under the slope
of the ground, for protection from the cannonade ; so
that this French column, in its advance, suffered from
a severe fire of artillery, and was at a very short
distance assailed by Maitland's brigade, which then
rose, and, being in a four-deep formation, was seen
for the first time by the French Guard.   Maitland's
brigade now opened a heavy and most destructive fire

upon the French Guard while in column, and the fire
from the right of Colin Halkett's brigade must also
have told upon that column, which soon got into utter
confusion and could not deploy.   Maitland's and part
of Halkett's brigade advanced upon it when in this
state of confusion, and drove it back in a state of rout.
Maitland's brigade was thrown into some confusion
by this advance, but both it and Halkett's right soon
resumed their proper position in the line in good
order.

The head of the left column of the French Guard
was now approaching the ground occupied by Maitland's brigade, bringing its front under the fire of
that brigade, while its whole left flank became exposed
to be attacked by Adam's brigade, as the left of that
brigade now stood to the right of the very small
remains of Byng's brigade, consequently a little to the
right of Maitland's brigade, and its right pointing
towards Hougoumont, in which position it stood at
some degree of angle with Maitland's brigade.  Colonel
Colborne, who commanded the left battalion of the
brigade, the 52nd Regiment (there were some companies of the 95th Rifles on his left), seeing that the
battalion would not be quite parallel to the flank of
the French column on its advance, ordered, on his own
authority, the left company of the battalion to wheel
about the eighth of the circle to its left, and formed
the others upon it in a line four deep.  This line he

covered by the right company thrown out in skirmishing order. When the French column was sufficiently advanced to have its left flank opposite to the front of the 52nd Regiment, its advance was checked first by the fire of the skirmishers of the 52nd, and then entirely stopped by the fire of the battalion. The discipline of the 52nd Regiment was at all times admirable ; and Colborne caused the movements on this occasion to be made with a precision which ensured coolness, gave security against all attack, and rendered both the firing and the advance in line of the battalion of the most formidable character.

138. The French column, feeling the severity of the fire of the 52nd, wheeled up its left sections and commenced firing ; but the fire from the 52nd threw it into great disorder, and the combined fire and formidable advance in line of the 52nd caused the entire rout and dispersion of the four battalions of the French Guard which were opposed to it. Colborne continued his advance in line, four deep, in a diagonal line from the point at which he defeated the French Guard, across the front of the position of the 1st and 3rd divisions, directing his march so that the left of the 52nd came upon the Charleroi road so near to the orchard of La Haye Sainte, that part of the 95th, that were on Colborne's left, got into the orchard. When the left of the 52nd reached the

Charleroi road, its right was still at some distance from that road; and Colborne, seeing three battalions of the enemy formed on the west side of that road, by a left-shoulder-forward movement brought his regiment parallel to the three battalions of the enemy, and advanced towards them and halted. These three battalions were of the Imperial Guard, but not composed of any part of the four battalions which the 52nd had previously defeated. They were part of the four battalions which were repulsed in their attack on the British Guards and Halkett's British brigade. They stood in three contiguous columns of battalions, the right resting on the Charleroi road, where that road forms a hollow way from passing through the ridge which is intermediate between the two ridges that formed the positions of the French and Anglo-Allied armies. When Colborne halted the 52nd, it was in line in its four-deep formation, and parallel to the heads of the three battalions of the French Guard to which it was opposed.

139. The Duke of Wellington rode forward in the line of the advance of the 52nd, reached that regiment, and, after examining the three battalions of the enemy in its front, ordered Colborne to attack them, remarking that they would not stand.

140. Colborne then advanced to the attack of those three battalions of the French Guard, and routed and dispersed them. This attack was made with the

same admirable steadiness and discipline as in the attack of the four battalions. Colborne now crossed to the left of the Charleroi road, and advanced, leaving La Belle Alliance and Trimotion to his right : a show of resistance was made by some companies of the enemy, but they soon fled, and the 52nd continued its march on the left of the Charleroi road to beyond Rossomme, when it again crossed to the right of the Charleroi road, and there the whole brigade joined and bivouacked for the night.

141. The march of the 52nd Regiment has thus been traced continuously, without referring to other incidents of the battle during its advance; for its progress was the leading and distinctive feature of the action during that period; and it will thus be more easy, by reference to the progress of the 52nd, to understand what was done by the rest of the Anglo-Allied army, and the Prussian army, during this most highly-interesting part of the action, and by this means to connect together a sufficiently complete view of the general state and progress of the battle, from the defeat of the columns of the Imperial Guard until the termination of the contest. This will best be done, and the coincidence of the events best shown, by stating what progress was made by the remainder of the Anglo-Allied army, and the three corps of the Prussian army, correspondingly with the advance of the 52nd.

142. It will be remembered that Adam's brigade
consisted of the 52nd Regiment, the 71st Regiment,
and the 2nd and 3rd battalions of the 95th Rifles.
In the advance of the 52nd it was accompanied on
its left by the 2nd battalion of the 95th, while, during
the whole of the advance of the 52nd, the 71st was in
its right rear; and on the right of the 71st was the
3rd battalion 95th Regiment.   When the 52nd crossed
the Charleroi road, after defeating the three battalions of the Imperial Guard, the 71st and 3rd
battalion of the 95th continued their advance on the
right of that road.   This partial separation of the
brigade arose from Colborne having taken upon
himself the responsibility of wheeling the 52nd to
its left, and attacking the four battalions of the
Guard.   It is perhaps impossible to point out in
history any other instance in which so small a
force as that with which Colborne acted had so
powerful an influence on the result of a great battle,
in which the numbers engaged on each side were so
large.

143. The effect of the defeat of the ten battalions
of the Imperial Guard, and of Colborne's diagonal
march, was electrical on Donzelot's division, which
was in fact compromised by the advance of Adam's
brigade.   Its attack, which had up to that time been
violently severe upon Alten's division, was at once
slackened and very soon suspended, and a retreat

commenced.    Simultaneously with the advance of
Adam's brigade after the defeat of the four battalions
of the Guard, General Hew Halkett advanced with
the Osnabruck battalion in pursuit of the two battalions of the Old Guard which were in rear and in
support of the four battalions; they retired in good
order, not having been quite sufficiently advanced to
receive the fire of Adam's brigade; but fell into considerable confusion when followed and attacked by
Halkett, who made prisoner General Cambronne,
who commanded them.    Halkett continued his advance to the Charleroi road, and by it ultimately
accompanied the Prussian advance to Genappe.

144. When Wellington saw that Adam's brigade,
and Hew Halkett with the Osnabruck battalion, were
advancing in pursuit of the defeated French Guard;
that Donzelot's and Alix's attacks were in consequence abated in intensity; that Zieten was advancing from Smohain and Papelotte; and that the
corps of Bülow and Pirch were fully engaged with
the enemy's right in the vicinity of Planchenoit,—
he ordered the advance of the whole Anglo-Allied
line, and, having done so, galloped forward to the
52nd Regiment, as already stated.

145. When Zieten's corps arrived on the left of
the Allied line, his cavalry rendered the presence
there of Vivian's and Vandeleur's cavalry brigades
no longer necessary; upon which, Vivian immedi-

ately put his brigade in march to its right, and
formed it in rear of that part of the position on
which Kielmansegge's and Ompteda's stood, and
which was now reinforced by the Brunswick and
some of the Nassau troops; this part of the line was
so severely pressed by the continued, close, and persevering attacks of the enemy, that the support of
Vivian's brigade at this point was of importance.
Vandeleur's brigade also marched to its right, and
was placed in support of that part of Chassé's Dutch-
Belgian division which stood in rear of the Guards.
When the Duke ordered the advance of the Anglo-
Allied line, Vivian's brigade advanced in a line
parallel to the direction of the Charleroi road, and
to the right of Adam's brigade; and Vandeleur
advanced in the same direction, to the right rear of
Vivian, and very near to the north-east end of the
Hougoumont enclosure. The advance of these two
brigades was spirited, and successful in clearing that
part of the field of the broken portions of the French
army which were still there; but which were, in
reality, in retreat.

146. The general advance of the Anglo-Allied
army caused the immediate retreat of the whole of
Donzelot's, Alix's, and Marcognet's divisions, and
the occupation of La Haye Sainte by Lambert's
brigade. On the right, the advance of the Anglo-
Allied troops from Hougoumont and its northern

enclosures drove the French from the wood of Hougoumont; and their right being threatened, they fell into continued retreat.

147. At the period of the advance of Adam's brigade by its diagonal march to the Charleroi road, Zieten's corps, having advanced from Smohain and Papelotte, was in contest with Durutte's division; and Bülow's and Pirch's divisions had renewed the attack on Drouot's corps on the French left of Planchenoit, while they at the same time violently attacked Planchenoit, and advanced also to turn it on the French right. These contests were most severe and bloody, and were in full vigour when the 52nd crossed the Charleroi road; the Prussian guns then reached to some parts of that road. The French defence of Planchenoit was so obstinate, that they still retained it; but the retreat of the defeated portion of the French Guard, and of D'Erlon's and Reille's corps (also in a state of rout), caused the retreat of Drouot's corps and of the Guard in and near to Planchenoit. The rout of the whole French army, in great disorder, was now complete; its loss in killed, wounded, and prisoners is not known, but was enormously great, and it lost nearly all its artillery. It was dissolved as an army. The Duke of Wellington, after seeing from a height near to Rossomme that the rout and retreat of the French army were complete, left the pursuit to the Prussian

army, and it was continued by them during the night. During this retreat the losses of the French army were great, and its dissolution as an army was completed.

148. When Wellington saw from Rossomme the whole of the French army in rout and in full retreat, Napoleon was a fugitive; and it may be considered that from that moment his military and political power ceased for ever. Wellington was, on the contrary, and continued to be for thirty-seven years —that is, during the whole of the remainder of his life—the greatest and most influential man in Europe, both as regards politics and war. The remainder of Napoleon's life was that of an unhappy exile on a distant and dreary spot which stood in the midst of the vast ocean. It was during this miserable period of his existence that he dictated those Memoirs, so little known and so much neglected in this country, which are superior in military views to those con- tained in any other composition which the world has ever yet seen.

149. There can now be no doubt that Napoleon, before he acted with the army of Italy in 1795—that is, when he was twenty-five years of age—had pro- foundly studied the science of war, and attained the greatest mastery of it by having made himself ac- quainted with all the known histories of the cam- paigns of the great commanders, both ancient and

modern. It is evident that, from his great powers
of mind, he had been able to see in them what was
defective; and that all which was good he seized
upon and classified, so as to fix in his mind so extensive a collection of principles as to enable him to
solve every case upon principle, however new or
complicated the case might be; and this, together
with his great natural capacity, appears to account
for the ready and grand solution which he gave to
every military question, whether on the field of
battle or in the cabinet. This rapidity and fixedness
of decision was, from the first time of his assuming
the command of an army, a matter of utter surprise
to the most experienced officers;—that any of them
fathomed the cause does not appear.

150. But there is an error, almost universal as
regards the bulk of mankind, in supposing that great
commanders, such as Napoleon, Wellington, Cæsar,
and Hannibal, did not commit great mistakes. The
game of war is so exciting, so complicated, and presents so many propositions which are capable of a
variety of solutions, and which must be solved irre-
vocably on the instant, that no human powers of
mind can reach further than a comparative excellence
as a great commander; that is, great commanders
will have higher views, act upon superior principles,
and commit fewer errors, than ordinary men; but
still this is only comparative merit, and should not

exempt the operations of even the greatest commanders from criticism. If those principles be admitted as being correct, the apparent presumption will be accounted for of pointing out what are here considered as decided mistakes committed by each of the great commanders, Napoleon and Wellington, at Waterloo.

151. The operations which Napoleon conducted and directed on the 17th of June, 1815, were so defective and so erroneous that they led to the catastrophe by which he was overwhelmed on the 18th. In fact, it must for ever appear almost incredible, to those who have made themselves acquainted with the history of Napoleon's previous campaigns, that his operations on the 17th of June should have been so tardy and defective. His operations up to the evening of the 16th had, in their general result, been successful by Blucher's being defeated and separated from Wellington; but to reap the fruits of his combinations and success over Blucher, it became necessary to strike against Wellington with the utmost rapidity and vigour; and it was impossible that circumstances could have been more favourable for his doing so than those which actually existed at daylight on the morning of the 17th. The Prussian army was in full retreat. Wellington's army (not yet fully collected) stood only seven or eight miles from Napoleon's; and Ney was in contact with Wel-

lington's front. Wellington's left was completely
exposed, and stood on the great chaussée, by which
chaussée Napoleon had the immense advantage of
being able to advance perpendicularly to the line of
the Anglo-Allied army, and thus to attack it to the
greatest advantage before it was by any means fully
in junction, and on its left flank at right angles to its
line of battle ; while, simultaneously with Napoleon's
attack on the left, Ney would have assailed Wellington's front.

152. But Napoleon, as if utterly infatuated, in
place of commencing his movement against Wellington at daylight, lost seven hours, which enabled
Wellington to withdraw from Quatre Bras without
loss, and to establish his whole army firmly in the
position of Waterloo on the evening of the 17th.

153. Napoleon strongly insists upon it that his
detaching 32,000 men to pursue the Prussian army
on the 17th was in conformity with the best principles of war, as otherwise Blucher might have returned
to Fleurus, and thus Napoleon would have lost his
line of communication. When Napoleon states as
one of the general principles of war—which he does
in many parts of his works—that losing his line of
communication is one of the greatest errors which a
general can commit, there can be nothing more true.
But in this case Napoleon would not have lost his
line of communication with France had Blucher im-

mediately reoccupied the position of Ligny upon
Napoleon's leaving it; for his advance upon Well-
ington necessarily opened to him both the Mons and
Lille great lines to France.

From the position in which Napoleon stood, both
political and military, his greatest object and aim
should have been the defeat of the Anglo-Allied
army, and he ought to have fallen upon it with his
whole force without a moment of unnecessary delay.
In this view, it is considered here as a vast error,
and as being entirely unsuited to the circumstances
in which he was placed, that Napoleon should have
detached 32,000 men in search of Blucher, who
had gone he knew not whither. Had Napoleon, in
place of detaching 32,000 men from his army, caused
Blucher's retreating columns to be followed by 4000
cavalry, Blucher's retreat would have been the same,
for he could not have ascertained, during the 17th,
what force was following him. But adopting the
most violent supposition, that of Blucher's immediate
return to Ligny, nothing else could have been so
favourable to Napoleon. He would then have been
opposite to the Anglo-Allied army with his whole
army in junction, have had two great lines of communication open with France, and have stood directly
between Wellington and Blucher; thus effectually and
completely separating them. Even had Blucher got

back to Ligny on the 17th—an almost impossible case
—he would have been so far from Waterloo as not to
have been able to reach it in rear of the French army
in time to act on the 18th in favour of Wellington; for
on the supposition that Napoleon had marched seven
hours earlier on the 17th from Ligny, he not only
must have caused a most serious loss to the Anglo-
Allied army, but would have formed his line of
battle that evening for the attack, and would therefore have attacked that evening or early next morning;
besides which, a rear-guard at Genappe could have
long delayed the whole Prussian army.   The critical
reader may doubt whether it is consistent reasoning
to say that Wellington would have suffered severely
in retreating from Quatre Bras had Napoleon attacked
him early on the morning of the 17th; and at the
same time to say that, had the Prussian army marched
upon Napoleon's rear on the 18th it would have
easily been much delayed by being opposed by a detachment of the French army; for, as it may be
argued, if the Duke could have checked the French
advance on the Dyle, a French detachment could
have checked Blucher's advance across that river to
support Wellington.   But it must be recollected that
if Wellington had attempted to oppose Napoleon on
the 17th on the Dyle, the immediate consequence
would have been a general action there before Well-

ington's own army was by any means in junction, against the whole French army, which would then have been in complete junction.

154. But the assertion that Napoleon's dividing his army was a vast error is founded upon higher and more important considerations. On the morning of the 17th of June he was operating with about 100,000 men against about 200,000 men; and it was manifestly and absolutely essential to him, in the military and political position in which he stood, to defeat, separate, and paralyze the armies of Wellington and Blucher, in order that he might have even the least chance of re-establishing himself on the throne of France. His great difficulty—as he ought well to have known from the experience of a whole succession of disastrous campaigns to his armies in Spain—was the overthrow of the Anglo-Allied army; and against it he should have led his last man and horse, even had the risk been great in the highest degree; which, as has been seen, it clearly was not. Had Napoleon attacked the Anglo-Allied army with his whole force, and succeeded in defeating it, there could be little question of his being able to defeat afterwards the Prussian army when separated from Wellington; so that, of all suppositions, the most favourable to Napoleon's ultimate success would be that of the Prussian army having attempted to intercept his line of communication; yet it is upon

this fallacious argument that Napoleon—with at least
an assumed sincerity—justifies so confidently the
division of his force : it will appear to most minds too
bold to say that Napoleon took a view of his case,
and position, below what the circumstances called for.
That the man who had by his genius and energy,
and the vastness of his views, gone far towards the
conquest of all Europe, should have failed to play a
great game in a case on which his whole fortunes
hinged, is certainly difficult to understand ; but it
must be borne in mind that there is a distinction
between vastness of views and the personal conduct
of operations ; and that it is not at all inconsistent
with sound views to suppose that, while a man was
rising to power, and throwing for empire first, and
then for conquest, he might be more fitted for playing
a desperate game than when acting a more defensive
part at a more advanced period of his career.  It was
necessary that Napoleon, under the circumstances,
should throw for entire success, and he failed to do
so ; this was acting a part incommensurate with the
circumstances in which he was placed ; for anything
short of complete success would have entailed his
ruin as certainly as a defeat would have done.  He
failed, therefore, in not playing a great enough
game.

155. That the 32,000 men detached by Napoleon
on the 17th of June did not act on the field of battle

in aid of Napoleon on the 18th has been attributed to the misconduct of the officer who commanded that force. If the preceding reasoning is correct, the original error rested upon Napoleon himself. It is argued by the supporters and admirers of Napoleon, that when Grouchy heard, at noon on the 18th of June, the heavy cannonade at Waterloo, he should have marched to the place from which that sound proceeded, as its severity indicated that a general action was in progress there. This is very plausible, and the argument rests on fair grounds; for on the day of a general and decisive battle, a lieutenant cannot be much out of place if he joins in the fight; and Grouchy could not have been said to be far wrong, and perhaps would have acted the best part, had he marched directly to the field of battle indicated by the cannonade; although contrary to his instructions, which were to march upon Blucher at Wavre. Had Grouchy acted upon the principle of directing his march by the sound of the artillery, his doing so would in all probability have produced little or no effect in favour of Napoleon on the field of Waterloo, from the following causes :—the length of the march, the state of the roads, the extreme intricacy of the country, and the opposition that Thielemann's corps would have offered. But the idea that Grouchy was entirely wrong, that the fault was entirely his, that his bungling or treason caused the loss of the action,

cannot be admitted as a portion of authentic history :
it has soothed French susceptibilities, and has been
employed to give a more favourable view of Napoleon's combinations.   In respect to the latter it utterly
fails, which may be shown by the following view,
which, so far as I know, has not hitherto been brought
forward ; but which, when stated, must, as I conceive,
be a self-evident proposition.   The allegation is, that,
when at noon Grouchy heard such a cannonade as to
indicate that a general action was in progress, he
ought to have marched directly to the field of battle.
Now, even admitting this to be true, it implies that
Napoleon committed the same error in a far stronger
and more inexcusable degree.   If Grouchy's proper
place was on the field of battle at Waterloo, then
Napoleon should have sent for him at daylight on
the morning of the 18th, when he saw the Anglo-
Allied army in position, and determined to attack it.
Napoleon knew with positive certainty that a general
action was taking place : if then the principle was
correct that Grouchy should take part in it, why did
not Napoleon order him to march upon Planchenoit ?
Napoleon had positive and certain knowledge of the
existence of a general action, and was free to give to
Grouchy what orders he chose ; Grouchy, on the contrary, only could guess as to the existence of a
general action, and in acting upon a probable supposition would have done so contrary to his instruc-

tions. Now Napoleon not only failed to send any order to Grouchy to march upon Waterloo, when he knew positively that he was about to engage in a general action with the Anglo-Allied army; but even when the action was actually commencing, he caused Soult to write to him, approving of his marching upon Wavre. If then Grouchy violated a principle in not marching to the field of battle, Napoleon violated the same principle, and in an aggravated degree, by not ordering his march upon Waterloo early on the morning of the 18th; and in going the length of approving of his march upon Wavre when the battle of Waterloo was actually commencing.

156. This error on the part of Napoleon may, at first sight, appear strange; but the correspondence and other documents make the cause sufficiently evident. It is clear that Napoleon did not at all foresee the movement of Blucher upon Waterloo, which is in fact proved positively by the report made by Grouchy to Napoleon, dated Gembloux, 17th June, ten o'clock P.M.; and by the order transmitted by Soult to Grouchy, from in front of the farm of Caillou, on the field of Waterloo, dated ten o'clock on the morning of the 18th June. By the former of these documents it is clearly shown that Grouchy considered that, by his advance upon Wavre, he would separate the Prussian force from

Napoleon; and this opinion of Grouchy Napoleon distinctly approved of, and confirmed, in the communication from Soult, dated ten o'clock A.M., from Caillon, in which the receipt of Grouchy's report, dated ten o'clock P.M. of the 17th, is acknowledged, and he is ordered to march direct upon Wavre, and drive before him any of the enemy he may find there; and he is desired, at the same time, to keep up his communication with Napoleon, which has been absurdly construed into an instruction to march towards Napoleon, while it simply and clearly meant that he should keep up his communication with Napoleon by patroles, as was evidently proper; and by no possible perversity of construction will it bear the other meaning, for the order is express and direct that Grouchy shall march to Wavre, and not only is this ordered, but that he should get there as rapidly as possible. One error Grouchy unquestionably did commit—that of not marching on the morning of the 18th till between eight and nine o'clock, in place of doing so at four A.M.; thus losing between four and five hours. But his having marched at four o'clock in the morning could not, by any possibility which I can see, have effected anything favourable to Napoleon on the field of Waterloo. Had Grouchy marched four or five hours earlier, his advance to Wavre, in place of being turned towards Waterloo, would have been much more certain.

Bülow's corps marched from Wavre at four o'clock on
the morning of the 18th, and was followed by that
of Pirch and that of Zieten; so that, had Grouchy
marched at four o'clock, he could only have found
Thielemann's corps at Wavre, the result from which
only could have been that of his pushing Thielemann
further back towards Brussels or Waterloo, but without the possibility of affording any aid to Napoleon;
and the more Grouchy advanced, the more he became
compromised, if Napoleon did not succeed in defeating the Allied army.

157. It is a matter of no doubt, therefore, but of
certainty, that neither Napoleon nor Grouchy took
at all into consideration the possibility of the march
of the whole Prussian army on the morning of the
18th from Wavre to join Wellington on the field of
Waterloo; and Soult's communication to Grouchy,
dated ten A.M. on the 18th, proves positively that
Napoleon had at that hour come to exactly the same
determination, as to the march to Wavre by Grouchy,
which Grouchy came to at twelve o'clock, Napoleon
having then a more positive knowledge than Grouchy
had of the existence of a general action, and Napoleon
not being fettered, as Grouchy was, by any contrary
order. It is perfectly clear, therefore, that Napoleon
in this matter acted under two erroneous impressions;
for, first, he had no idea that the whole Prussian army
was to be put in motion against him from Wavre on

M 2

the morning of the 18th ; and, second, he had the full
and confident conviction that he was strong enough,
with the army he had with him at Waterloo on the
morning of the 18th, to defeat and destroy the army
of Wellington.    This is proved by the exultation
which he expressed at the time at Wellington's
having committed the error of halting to be attacked,
and by the opinion which he afterwards expressed,
that, if Wellington had been defeated, he must have
been destroyed by having the forest of Soignies in
his rear.    As to this second alleged error, it may be
said that it has not been proved that he was wrong
in supposing that he would have defeated Wellington,
had Wellington not been supported by the Prussians.
But this does not materially affect the question, it
having been clearly proved that, even had the result
been ultimately favourable to Napoleon, the struggle
would have been so desperate, and the loss on both
sides so enormous, that Napoleon's calculation was
erroneous in not having brought against Wellington
every man and horse that it was possible for him to
collect.

158. The forest of Soignies, which Napoleon re-
presents as a défilé that would have caused tho ruin
of the Anglo-Allied army in the event of its defeat,
is penetrated by several roads, and, not having under-
wood, would have been a great protection to the
Anglo-Allied army had it been defeated, and followed

in its retreat by the magnificent force of cavalry which was with Napoleon.

159. The order of battle in which Napoleon formed his army on the morning of the 18th of June, opposite to and with the view of attacking that of Wellington, was so excellent, that it will probably always be considered as a model for study in the consideration of such formations. Napoleon had the disadvantage of this formation being in some degree deranged, even early in the action, by the force detached from the centre to observe the Prussian advance; and later in the action this disadvantage became more and more serious. The mode in which Napoleon directed the progress of this great action must, of course, to military men, be a subject of the greatest interest as a military study. The first question which arises is the propriety, or otherwise, of his having made his first two attacks merely isolated attacks; the first being alone upon Hougoumont, and the second upon the left only of the Anglo-Allied line. Such isolated attacks cannot, it is here presumed, be considered as otherwise than as very defective operations. The third attack was not only defective from being a merely partial attack on the centre of the Anglo-Allied army, but was in the highest degree objectionable by being made only by cavalry. In fact, this third attack, made by the whole of his magnificent force of heavy cavalry, was an error of surpassing magni-

tude on the part of Napoleon, because, first, it was a merely isolated attack ; second, it was made by cavalry alone ; third, it was made on a portion of the Anglo-Allied army which had not before been attacked at all, and consequently not in the least degree broken or exhausted ; and fourth, it was a premature period of the action at which to attempt to decide the battle by a mere charge of cavalry.   No part of Wellington's line of battle was at that period of the action either so exhausted, or so shaken, as to warrant the supposition that his order of battle could be overthrown by cavalry alone.   Napoleon, perfectly aware that this attack by his cavalry was in violation of principle, endeavours to throw the responsibility of its having been made upon others ; but this explanation cannot be received, for the movement was made actually under his view, and he had abundance of time to have stopped it, either by riding to the spot himself, or by means of his staff.   The movement was so distinctly seen from the ground occupied by the 3rd division, that this is stated with confidence.   Even upon the supposition that the first charge by forty squadrons had been made contrary to Napoleon's wish, why, when he saw that it failed, did he not stop the renewal of the attack ?   It may possibly have been the case that Napoleon did not commit so gross an error as to originate this attack, but that, on its being begun with so much spirit and confidence by his

magnificent cavalry, he allowed himself to be led
away by the hope of its securing victory before the
arrival of more of the Prussian army.   In this hope
he was fatally deceived; his cavalry was wrecked
and nearly destroyed, two hours were lost, and the
result was a greatly diminished chance of victory.

160. In his fourth and fifth attacks Napoleon
struck most perseveringly and most determinedly for
victory, and in a way more worthy of his great talents
and of his knowledge of war.   But that he conducted
his last grand attack, when the Guard was employed,
in the manner most likely to be attended with success,
cannot be admitted.   Not only La Haye Sainte, but
the ground in front of it up to within sixty yards of
the Allied line, was then in his possession.   Hougoumont had resisted successfully all attacks.   The
obvious mode, therefore, of conducting the last attack,
was that of bringing forward the Guard under the
protection of La Haye Sainte, close to the Anglo-
Allied line, and to have launched it upon that part of
the line, while D'Erlon's corps attacked to the right of
the Guard on the French right of the Charleroi road,
and Reille's to the left of the Guard between it and
the Hougoumont enclosures—the wood of Hougoumont being merely occupied, and Hougoumont itself
shelled.   Napoleon does not appear in this action to
have himself watched sufficiently narrowly its actual
progress.   His having failed to do so, and his having

acted on the report of others, may account for his having committed errors on a field of battle, and thus justify criticism.

161. A loose charge of having been surprised by Napoleon has been repeated against Wellington and Blucher. But it was made in ignorance, and easily repelled. That they were not surprised is quite certain, for they knew of Napoleon's having left Paris, of the march of the Guard, and of the movements of the French troops that were in Vivian's front, quite in time to have enabled them to assemble their armies before Napoleon passed the frontier. They acted on a different principle, and determined to continue in the cantonments which they occupied until they knew positively the line of attack. Now it may safely be predicted that this determination will be considered, by future and dispassionate historians, as a great mistake; for, in place of waiting to see where the blow actually fell, the armies should have been instantly put in motion to assemble. Nor was this the only error: the line of cantonments occupied by the Anglo-Allied and Prussian armies was greatly too extended. Blucher's left was at Liége, and Wellington's right at Audenarde, a distance of upwards of 100 English miles in a direct line, as measured on the map; the distance by the same measurement, from Liége to the Charleroi road to Brussels, is nearly 60 miles by cross-roads; and from Audenarde

to that road is 40 miles; and the distance from Thuin,
behind which the French army might all form within
the French frontier, is only 40 English miles from
Brussels.   This absurd extension of the cantonments
of the Anglo-Allied and Prussian armies made it
certain that, if Napoleon succeeded in assembling his
army unperceived by his opponents, he could separate
the Anglo-Allied and Prussian armies from each
other and attack them separately; which proves,
beyond all doubt, that their line of cantonments was
dangerous and defective, and it was made greatly
more so by the audacious manner in which, without
any due calculation of time and distances, three corps
of the Prussian army were kept so far in advance of
the direct line between Blucher's extreme left at Liége
and Wellington's right at Audenarde.   The head-
quarters of the 1st corps was Charleroi, of the 2nd
Namur, of the 3rd Ciney; and these corps extended
to Lobbes and Thuin on the Sambre, and to Dinant
on the Meuse.

162. The French army had the choice of five routes
by which to advance to the attack of Wellington and
Blucher.   First, from the frontier near Lille, by Audenarde and Ninove, upon Brussels.   Second, from the
frontier near to Lille and Condé, upon Ath, Enghien,
and Hal, upon Brussels.   Third, from the frontier
near to Maubeuge, by Mons, Soignies, and Hal.
Fourth, from the frontier near to Beaumont, by

Charleroi, Gosselies, and Genappe, and Binch and
Nivelles, and the forest of Soignies, upon Brussels.
Fifth, from the frontier near to Charlemont and Givet,
upon Namur and Louvain.   From the time, therefore,
that it became known that Napoleon's army was
organised and formed into corps ready to take the
field, the armies of Wellington and Blucher should
have been so placed in cantonments as to be prepared
to meet any of the cases supposed by a junction of
their whole forces upon any of the lines of attack
which Napoleon might adopt, without leaving even
a possibility of their being attacked separately; and
from the moment that it was known that the French
army was at all in movement, the Allied armies should
have been withdrawn from cantonments and placed
very near to each other.

163. Had Napoleon advanced by the second, by
the third, or by the fourth road above named, it is
quite clear that it was impossible that the Allied
armies could have been in junction at any point
between him and Brussels, so as to have covered it
by opposing to him their whole united force in a
general action.   Each of the distances from Liége
and Ciney to the nearest parts from them of the
Genappe road is greater than Napoleon's whole
march would have been to Brussels; yet the Genappe
road is the nearest of the three to the cantonments
which were occupied by the Prussian army.  A super-

ficial observer would reply, that it cannot be true that the Allied armies could not have concentrated in time to oppose Napoleon before he reached Brussels, as they actually did so at Waterloo; but the proposition implies that Napoleon's advance, as supposed, must have obliged the Allies, if they opposed him before he reached Brussels, to do so without having the whole of their force in junction; and this is what took place, and certainly at an imminent risk of being attended with most disastrous results.

164. As to the first and fifth of the lines by which Napoleon might have advanced, they were not sufficiently direct to suit his position, respect being had to the other armies by which he was threatened; and they were objectionable as strategical lines, and therefore did not require so much attention as the other three.

165. But as most decided objection has been made here to the dispositions of the Allied armies previous to the actual commencement of hostilities, it is necessary to go into the question of what ought to have been their line of cantonments as soon as it was known that Napoleon had a large organised army ready to take the field; and what position they should have taken up when it became known that the French army was in motion, so as to render it certain that Napoleon could not bring a portion of the Allied army into action with his concentrated force; and

that he could only reach Brussels after an overthrow
of the whole of the Allied army when in junction, in
a general action.    We say that the first of these
cases would have been completely met by Blucher's
having made Genappe his head-quarters, cantonning
his army between Louvain and Gosselies, occupying
the line of the Sambre from Namur to the frontier
by strong bodies of cavalry, and having advanced
posts of cavalry along the frontier on that front; and
by Wellington having his head-quarters at Brussels,
cantonning his army from Brussels to Soignies, with
cavalry outposts along the frontier from the right of
Blucher's outposts to the Scheldt, and then along that
river to Audenarde.    The second case would have
been met by Blucher's army being assembled at
Genappe, and Wellington's at Hal.

166. The determination of Wellington and Blucher
to meet Napoleon's advance at Fleurus and Quatre
Bras was totally inconsistent with the widely
scattered positions in which they had placed their
armies; their determination in this respect amounted
in the fullest extent to that error which has so
often been committed in war, by even great commanders, of endeavouring to assemble on a point
which could only be reached by a portion of the
troops intended to occupy it, while the enemy had
the power of concentrating upon it his whole force.
Even upon the suppositions above, of the cantonments

having been concentrated to the parallelogram indicated by lines joining Louvain, Brussels, Soignies,
and Gosselies ; or the still greater concentration into
camp ; the Allies should not have accepted battle
beyond the left bank of the Dyle. The totally
inadequate reason for not concentrating the armies
was a mere alleged inconvenience as to supplies ;
in other words, two armies fully prepared with all
their means of taking the field, in the richest country
in Europe, and with their communications both by
sea and land completely open, were, for this mere
supposed inconvenience, to risk being destroyed in
detail by an inferior army. If the Allied armies
had been in this helpless state as to the means of
subsistence, they would have been totally unequal
to manœuvre as an army in junction in face of
an enemy.

167. There can be no doubt that, so long as history
is read, the battle of Waterloo will be much and
eagerly discussed ; and that, so long as the art of war
is studied, its great features, and most important
details, will form subjects of anxious inquiry and
consideration by military men. It seems right,
therefore, in the face of all the accusations of presumption which must arise against any one who
criticises the military operations of Wellington and
Napoleon, that those who saw the operations, who
were in a position to know some of the important

details, and who have read all the published accounts
of importance up to this date (November, 1858),
should state what they know, and give their
opinions, so that the facts may be added to, and
the subject shown in different views. For these
reasons I shall continue these criticisms somewhat
further, so as to bring under review again a few of
the most important points of the action.

168. Wellington certainly ought to have had
Colville, with the force under his command, on the
field of battle at Waterloo. There was no cause
whatever for his being kept in the direction of Hal.
It would have been a gross error on the part of
Napoleon to have detached any important force on
that road, and Colville should, early on the morning
of the 18th, have been ordered to march to Waterloo
if he had no information of the advance of the enemy
on Hal.

169. The most important mistake which the Duke
of Wellington committed as to the actual fighting
of the battle of Waterloo, was his overlooking the
vast importance of retaining possession, at any cost,
of the farm and enclosures of La Haye Sainte.
This farm was at the very centre of his position,
and was on the great chaussée by which the
French army so easily approached the position; these
circumstances, and Napoleon's known modes of
attack, indicated that the possession of this farm

would be of the utmost value. Napoleon had from the first seen the vast importance of his possessing himself of this part of Wellington's field of battle, as is proved by his massing so very large a force immediately opposite to it, and by his establishing a battery of 74 guns to bear upon it. Lord Ellesmere says that the Duke, with that noble singleness of mind by which, among his other great qualities, he was so eminently distinguished, acknowledged his having been in error as to La Haye Sainte ; and he admitted what was certainly true, for its importance was such, that in place of being neglected, and all the implements removed from it, by which preparations might have been made for its defence (and which also had the effect of lulling all supposition that it was to be defended), it ought on the contrary to have been occupied, in addition to Baring's weak battalion, by one of the weak British battalions ; and all the usual means of defence should have been in progress during the whole night of the 17th and morning of the 18th. The proposals for strengthening the place on the morning of the 18th were repudiated by the head-quarter staff. When it was seen in the morning that a general action was inevitable, it was suggested to them to place a British battalion in the buildings in addition to Baring's, but the proposal was negatived.

That Napoleon from the first attached much more

importance than Wellington did to the possession
of that part of the Anglo-Allied position at which
La Haye Sainte stood, is fully proved by his having
prepared such immense means for its attack; while
Wellington occupied the ground weakly and para-
lyzed the defence of the buildings by withdrawing
from them the workmen and tools that would have
been required to put them into a state of defence.
In this instance, as in that of the dispositions of
the armies when the operations of the campaign
were commencing, Napoleon's general views seem
to have been superior to those of Wellington; but
in both cases Wellington showed great superiority in
execution. The blunders and looseness of Napoleon's
movements on the 16th, 17th, and 18th were sur-
passingly great and numerous; while Wellington
acted with unerring energy, firmness, and precision.
His ready boldness in making the stand which he
did at Waterloo, and in arranging that Blucher
should support him there, has seldom been surpassed.
Again, on the field of battle Wellington's execution
greatly surpassed that of Napoleon. Wherever there
was a turning-point in the battle, there Wellington
directed in person, judged for himself, and met the
storm. Napoleon, on the contrary, sluggishly kept
almost to one spot, and acted on the information of
others; for example, he says that he disapproved
of the great cavalry attack as a premature movement.

Why, then, when he saw Milhaud's whole corps of cavalry begin to move across the Charleroi road, immediately in front of where he stood, and directly under his view, did he not gallop forward with his staff and stop the movement? It was an isolated movement, so that he had at that moment nothing else calling for his immediate attention. Again, after the taking of La Haye Sainte, which uncovered the Anglo-Allied centre, in place of seeing, himself, what progress his troops had made there, and the state of the Anglo-Allied line at that critical point, he never took any close view of that, nor indeed of any other part of the action, and from this probably arose his giving an erroneous direction to the Guard when he finally struck for victory by ordering it to attack. Upon the whole, there seems fair reason to infer, that, like Cæsar, Wellington was ready, at all periods of his career, to throw for victory, at all hazards, with a coolness and self-possession that nothing could shake; while Napoleon, in his latter campaigns, fell more into a habit of trusting to his general directions: hence the general inference is probably not far from being correct, that, while Napoleon perhaps exceeded all men in general views in war, he did not display on all occasions the imperturbable moral firmness, combined with the utmost personal energy, that seem never for a moment to have been wanting in Cæsar and Wellington.

N

170. That the manner in which Napoleon formed his army for the attack, and that in which Wellington formed his for the defence of the position of Waterloo, were each masterpieces, cannot be doubted ;—and the determination, energy, perseverance, and skill, with which they so long struggled for victory, were admirable in both ; and prove how much the chances of victory would be against a less resolute and able general, if opposed by a great commander.

171. Napoleon was certainly deceived in this action, by his never having allowed himself to believe to its true extent in the tenacity with which a British army holds the ground that it is ordered to defend. This was no doubt the real cause of his allowing the premature charges by his cavalry upon the British line of infantry, which ended in the total wreck of that magnificent cavalry. Nor could he bring himself to believe that any line of infantry would endure the length and severity of the cannonade, and the attacks of cavalry and infantry, which he was able to direct against the Anglo-Allied line. In fact, the surpassing and extraordinary tenacity of the British infantry was beyond all calculation, beyond all praise, and was the sheet-anchor by which the Duke was enabled to ride out the storm. Full scope was thus given for the British cavalry and artillery to display their surpassing gallantry and excellence, and they did

not fail to display those qualities in an eminent degree. The King's German Legion were also troops of very great excellence; but the British and King's German Legion troops, actually in the action, were alarmingly few in number. I do not consider that any adequate idea can have been formed as to the battle of Waterloo by any one who does not come to the conclusion, that its result would have been eminently imperilled had the Duke of Wellington fallen in the action at any period of it previous to the last general attack. Having stated this opinion, it will be evident that the errors or shortcomings in the Duke's operations and in his guidance of the battle are only dilated upon here, as astronomers dilate upon the spots on the face of sun.

# SCHEME

FOR

# THE DEFENCE OF CANADA.

### WRITTEN IN FEBRUARY, 1862.

1. IN forming a plan for the defence of a country, it is necessary to take into consideration the extent of its population (upon which mainly the plan for its defence should be based)—its political position—its geography—and a proper application of military principles.

2. The information in regard to Canada on the above points may be cavilled at as to its precise accuracy, but for what is required for laying down the general principles that may be adopted for the defence of that country it is ample. This is particularly the case as to military views, as there are manuscripts by military men of great reputation and experience, entering very fully into the subject of the defence of Canada. Besides these private memoirs, there are some publications containing military views on the subject.

3. The observation will at once occur to every one, that the existence of the memoirs alluded to should form the groundwork of any plan now proposed for the defence of Canada. But this, it is held here, would be coming to a totally erroneous conclusion, for the following reasons. The warlike operations that had taken place in Canada before the memoirs alluded to were written, took place when the population of Canada was very small, and the armies by which the country was attacked were such as would now be considered utterly insignificant. In addition to this, the great principle of defending a country by great intrenched camps, partly occupied by a numerous militia and volunteer force, although not completely disciplined, was not then thought of, but is now forming a main feature of some of the best defen-

sive systems in Europe. The proposed plans for the defence of
Canada, in the military memoirs and plans already alluded to,
are generally clogged with the great fault of the suggested
occupation of numerous small fortified posts, having little
strength in themselves, and not being so placed as to connect a
great general system for the defence of the country. A few
observations by the Duke of Wellington on the defence of Canada
show that he had considered the subject with care, as is evident
from the sagacity and extent of view which they display; but
they lose much of their practical use by the case not being before
him of the very large armies that will now be employed, both
in the attack and defence, should the conquest of Canada be
attempted by the Federal States of North America.

4. Canada has now a population of about three millions of
souls. Of every population, one-tenth is capable of bearing arms,
allowing amply for all necessary deductions. Canada may, therefore, have under arms 300,000 men as volunteers and militia.
But we shall adopt here the supposition that if seriously attacked
she organizes a force of 130,000 men, and that this force is
supported by a British force of 30,000 men, making the whole
force for the defence of Canada 160,000 men. That this force can
be employed for the defence of Canada is now become certain
from the display of attachment to British connection which has
been made by Canada, and from the great military power of this
country. It is upon the supposition that some such force as
160,000 men will defend Canada, and that the attacking force is,
say, 200,000 men, that the defence of that country will be considered here.

5. So far as we know, it has never entered into the minds of
those who have hitherto written on the defence of Canada that
the attacking force would amount to anything like so large a
number as 200,000 men; but now few will doubt that, if Canada
is attacked at all, the attacking force will not fall short of that
number. A contrary opinion would imply a manifest absurdity;
for the strength of Canada, supported by Britain, has now proved
plainly, and undeniably, that 200,000 men can be displayed in
the defence of Canada; and we hold that it would be absurd to

suppose that an enemy would undertake such a conquest with an army smaller than what he would meet in the field; aided as the defending force would be by selected positions, fortifications, and the aids afforded by a population hostile to the invader. The preparations, therefore, in Canada should be on no smaller scale than that of opposing a force of 200,000 men under the following modification :—One of three states of things may result from what was the United States of North America: the Union may be restored—the Confederates and Federalists may separate and continue to have each much the same territory as at present —or the Confederates may succeed in separating themselves from the Federalists, and the latter split into further subdivisions. Now it is only in the latter case that Canada would be free from the liability of being attacked by the large force supposed ; and hence the necessity for placing that country in a permanent state of security; and a general plan for doing so is attempted to be laid down in the following observations.

6. The numerically very large force that will be employed in the defence of Canada at once suggests the idea of defending the country not only by an active and aggressive employment of that force, but by the employment of great intrenched camps, by which the complete security of the most important points of the country may be insured, and under the protection of which portions of the defensive force may find security when that is required. The great strategical and otherwise important points proposed here to be defended by intrenched camps are Montreal, Kingston, and Hamilton, including Burlington Heights, and permanent posts should be established at Sorel, Amherstburgh, Sarnia, and Penetangushene, which six places, together with Quebec, would, according to what is here proposed, form the only permanent works for the defence of Canada. But to defend even those places completely by permanent works would be highly expensive, and is not required. To exemplify this, suppose that it is determined to defend Montreal by a great intrenched camp : to do so by permanent works of masonry alone would require, say, ten such works on the N.W. side, and say seven on the opposite side of the St. Lawrence and on the islands. Now, supposing

each of those forts to be calculated to contain 450 men and 42 guns, and to cost the same as similar works made at Portsmouth, we may estimate the cost of each at 100,000*l.* as the contract price of a similar work at Portsmouth was 80,000*l.* Seventeen works of masonry, therefore, of the same dimension and character supposed, would cost 1,700,000*l.*

7. Now it is considered here that only eight such works are required for the permanent defence of Montreal; that is, to place that great and most important city in a state of safety against any attack which can be directed against it.

8. The opinion seems to have been generally adopted that the situation of Montreal is such that its being secured against attack by defensive works is extremely difficult. But this idea is considered here as being altogether erroneous, when its defence is considered under the supposition of its being formed into a great intrenched camp, and occupied by a numerous force, although the great proportion of that force is not highly disciplined. For determining upon the exact situation and plan of each work forming such an intrenched camp, the ground must be minutely examined by officers of Engineers who are capable of judging, not only of works, but of fields of battle. But the general outline may be sufficiently indicated from the plans of the ground. The line proposed here to be occupied by works for the defence of Montreal on its north and west side would commence where the Lachine Canal joins the St. Lawrence, above Montreal, and running northward would include Montreal Mountain; and from that mountain to very high ground; that is, to the west of, and in the direct line of the street called St. Denis; and to be continued from that high ground to a cut in the ground, 2700 yards further down than the high ground that is in a line in prolongation of St. Denis Street; and then turning to the east, at right angles to its former line, join the St. Lawrence; thus forming the termination below Montreal of the whole defensive line on the left bank of the St. Lawrence. This line extends nearly ten English miles, and would require ten forts of the strength supposed for its complete defence; but there can be no necessity for that number of permanent works of masonry—five would be sufficient, one of which

might be placed so as to secure the mountain, and two others to secure the highest and most important of the adjoining heights, and one on each flank of those heights, that is one between those heights and the termination of the line of defence above Montreal, and the other between those heights and the terminus of the line of defence below Montreal. Five other works, which would be redoubts of earth for the same number of men and guns each as the forts in masonry, and connecting lines by ditch and parapet, would complete the line of defence on the left bank of the St. Lawrence : the earthworks only to be made when attack is imminent. It is to be observed that, although the forts and redoubts proposed are each supposed to be for 450 men and 42 guns, this is liable to modification. The engineer would adapt each work to the ground, and some might be larger and some smaller; but the average strength of the works might be maintained so as to render the total cost the same. It is evident that when a number of forts are named, such as in the present case of five being named for the line north and west of Montreal, the forts occupying the high grounds might vary in size and form, according to the comparative importance of the heights to be occupied, and yet the general expense of the works might remain the same.

9. For the defence of the river side of Montreal, it is proposed that two forts in masonry shall be constructed on the right bank of the St. Lawrence, and one on the island called Nuns' Island or Châteauguay Island, at the mouth of the Châteauguay river, and that the islands of St. Helen's, St. Paul, and St. Thérèse, be occupied by earthworks; leaving the defence of the city on its river front to temporary expedients in case of actual operations being commenced against the place, or of such being imminent.

10. It is proposed that two forts in masonry be built on the right bank of the St. Lawrence, placed as follows :—Suppose a semicircle drawn, of which the diameter is 1000 yards, and its centre the point on the south bank at which that bank is cut by the Victoria Bridge, the fort would be on the circumference of that semicircle at a point of it immediately south of where it cuts the Grand Trunk Railway; and, when required, two

redoubts in earth would be made on the same semi-circumference, each about half-way between the permanent fort and the river on opposite sides of the railroad; and the whole three works would be joined by a ditch and parapet, strengthened as much as possible by the usual auxiliary means—thus forming a *tête-de-pont* of about 3000 yards of front, and of very great strength, so long particularly as the command of the river is maintained, which it is assumed here always would be the case. The other permanent fort, proposed to be on the right bank of the river, is supposed to be placed close to the north side of the Montreal and Portland Railroad, 1100 yards from the end of the pier that enters the St. Lawrence at the termination of that railway. Then, taking the end of the pier as a centre, and with a radius of 1100 yards cutting the bank of the river above that, and drawing a straight line to that point from the permanent fort, the situation of the redoubt in earth (when required) would be at the most favourable point of that line, and the line itself be that of a ditch and parapet. A ditch and parapet would also connect the permanent fort with Longueuil, and a redoubt in earth (when required) be constructed close to the north-east point of Longueuil, and Longueuil itself fortified strongly in the sense in which villages are occupied in field operations. This would form another very strong *tête-de-pont* of very nearly the same extent of front as the other; and the two would command 8000 yards of the south bank of the St. Lawrence, so as to form not only a great protection to the south side of the city, but give a formidable aggressive power on that side of the river, and make any attempt at investment on that side very difficult, and the successful investment of the city on both sides of the St. Lawrence scarcely possible. The 70,000 men proposed for defending Montreal are supposed to be placed as follows : 50,000 men for the defence of the ten miles of intrenched camp on the north and west of the city—6000 men to defend the two *têtes-de-ponts* on the right bank—450 men in the fort on the island at the mouth of the Châteauguay ; leaving 13,550 men to occupy redoubts in the islands and as a reserve force.

11. It is proposed above to have eight forts of masonry for the defence of Montreal, of an aggregate strength such as to contain

each a garrison of 450 men and 42 guns, each to be such a work as to require a regular siege operation for its reduction. When single works are named, such is meant to be their strength, but this must not be understood to imply that the engineer is not to employ his discretion as to the exact size and form of each work according to his judgment and skill; but when any number of permanent forts are named, it is meant that the engineer shall be limited to confining their aggregate extent to that named; for instance, that the five forts of masonry named for the defence of the north and west side of Montreal might, if thought expedient, be increased in number, but that still their total strength shall be such as to have a garrison of 2250 men and an armament of 210 heavy guns. When forts are named in these observations, permanent works in masonry are meant, of such strength as to have each a garrison of 450 men, and to be armed with 42 heavy guns; and when redoubts are named, field-works of earth are meant, having the same strength of garrison, and mounting the same number of guns, as the permanent forts. And it is further to be understood that, when any number of permanent forts are proposed for any place, the supplemental redoubts in earth are supposed to be made in such number that there shall be one work, whether fort or redoubt, on each mile of the front to be defended, be that front of what form it may. When the line to be defended is made continuous by connecting the forts and redoubts, it is always supposed to be done by a ditch and parapet of the same profile as the redoubt. These preliminary explanations will enable us to state, in a very few lines, what further forts in masonry we propose for the defence of Canada—which will also necessarily point out the number of redoubts required to fill up the ground to be occupied.

12. Two forts to be made at Sorel, one on the left bank of the river Richelieu, and the other on the right bank a little in advance of the town, between the right bank of the Richelieu and the bank of the St. Lawrence below Sorel; keeping in view that the two forts should completely command the Richelieu, here only 250 yards wide: these two forts, together with the field-works that

could be made when required, should be formed into an intrenched camp for 3000 men.

13. There are at present Fort Henry and some other works at Kingston for the protection of the entrance into the harbour. It is proposed here that four forts shall be built on the circumference of a semicircle drawn round the town on the land side, of such extent, that when the circumference of the semicircle is fully occupied with forts and redoubts, and their connecting lines, there would be formed a great intrenched camp for 25,000 men.

14. It is proposed that at Hamilton there shall be four forts built, so placed that, when necessary, with addition of redoubts and connecting lines, a great intrenched camp may be formed for 30,000 men, in such a way as to protect the town of Hamilton, to hold the position of Burlington Heights, and to secure the harbour.

15. The other permanent works proposed are:—one fort at Mississaga,—one fort at Amherstburgh,—one fort at Sarnia,—and one fort at Penetangushene.

16. The whole of the permanent works, therefore, here proposed for the defence of Canada,—in addition to those now existing,—are twenty-two forts of masonry, to be of the character and capacity already stated. As already stated, the force by which Canada is supposed to be defended is 160,000 men; and that force is supposed to be placed as follows:—7000 men at Quebec, 3000 men at Sorel, 70,000 men at Montreal, 25,000 men at Kingston, 23,000 men at Toronto, 30,000 men at Hamilton, 450 men at Mississaga, 450 men at Amherstburgh, 450 men at Sarnia, and 450 men at Penetangushene.

17. Having pointed out the situations for the permanent forts of masonry, and stated the number of men proposed for the defence of Canada, we shall proceed to state the principles upon which the scheme of defence now proposed is founded; this will include, in a general sense, the handling of the troops. The frontier of Canada extends in a straight line 750 miles from Quebec to River Detroit, which may be considered a continuous

front of battle, as the country has no depth to retire upon; consequently the line is liable to be cut at any point assailed. This great defect has to be considered and provided for, and it is proposed here to meet it by a system of great intrenched camps, under which the field forces may maintain themselves on certain highly important points, should they at any time lose, temporarily, the command in the field.

18. The situations proposed for those great intrenched camps are—Quebec, Sorel, Montreal, Kingston, and Hamilton. No additional permanent works have been proposed at Quebec, as an intrenched camp in earthworks of great strength, and of any required extent, could easily be made when required between the St. Lawrence and St. Charles rivers, having the present permanent works as the citadel.

19. Probably the most formidable attack that can be anticipated as being likely to be made upon Canada is that of 100,000 men acting against Montreal, and at the same time 100,000 men passing at the Niagara and Detroit frontiers, and directing their operations so as to converge towards Hamilton and Toronto. In this case the attacking force might have a temporary command in the field on both scenes of operation. To meet this state of things, 70,000 men would occupy the intrenched camp of Montreal; 25,000 that of Kingston; and 30,000 that of Hamilton; while 23,000 men from Toronto, and 5000 men from Quebec and Sorel, proceeded to assist in the defence of Montreal, by attacking in rear that portion of the enemy's forces that formed the investment on the left bank of the St. Lawrence; and thus cutting off completely their supplies. The action of this relieving force, together with vigorous, powerful, and well-concerted sorties made every morning at daylight, upon particular points of the enemy's necessarily very extended line of investment, would, if vigorously carried out, soon reduce him so that he would lose entirely the command in the field, and consequently be placed in a situation of peril.

20. The enemy's forces from the Niagara and Detroit frontier would find work enough before them in the intrenched camps of

Hamilton and Kingston, which camps they could not take but by some extremely tedious process of attack, if at all. The great strength of these camps would enable their defenders to make such a stand as to give ample time for their being relieved; so they could not be taken; nor durst an enemy, although 100,000 strong, pass 53,000 men in position, leaving them to act upon his rear, and with a hostile population round him.

21. If, then, this, the most formidable of all attacks upon Canada that it seems admissible to suppose, is to be defeated by the means that have been pointed out, a very moderate degree of skill will be required to defeat, with the same defensive means, less serious attacks.

22. There is much difficulty in laying down a satisfactory plan for defending that large and rich country included in a line drawn from Toronto to Lake Simcoe,—from Lake Simcoe to Georgian Bay,—then bounded by that bay, Lake Huron, the St. Clair river, the Lake St. Clair, the river Detroit, Lake Erie, the river Niagara, and the western point of Lake Ontario. The plan here suggested is that of having a camp of 30,000 men, the head-quarters of which should be at Hamilton, but having ten thousand men in a strongly intrenched camp at Thorald, and fort at Mississaga; having a camp for 23,000 men at Toronto, with 5000 men detached towards Stratford and London on the lines of railroad, and pointing towards the forts at Amherstburgh and Sarnia. By these arrangements, should an enemy cross the Niagara frontier in small force, he would be liable to immediate attack; and should he do so in large force, those advanced forces could be immediately withdrawn, or immediately supported. It will be observed, not only that there are railroads on those lines, but that those railroads are secure against any attack by an enemy, so that the defending force could be moved with great rapidity, until after the enemy had possessed himself of the country, and destroyed the railroads. If required, 50,000 men could, by the arrangements proposed, be assembled at any desired point of the fine country of which the boundaries have been named, still leaving all the forts fully

occupied, so that the rich country in question would be well secured against all kinds of attack, except by such a force as could defeat 50,000 men in position.

23. The question may be raised whether the four single forts proposed at Mississaga, Amherstburgh, Sarnia, and Penetan-gushene are required. After considering the subject, with every wish to dispense with them, we think that this cannot be done with safety. They seem necessary holds on those most distant parts of the country—points which the active force could operate upon with the certainty of finding supplies and military stores; and as points of communication with the naval forces that may be on Lakes Ontario, Erie, Huron, and the Georgian Bay of Lake Huron.

24. Obtaining and maintaining the command of the lakes and rivers of Canada is a matter of paramount importance as regards the defence of that country. It has been assumed in the preceding observations, that the command at sea, and of the St. Lawrence as high up as Montreal—including Lake St. Louis—is completely and fully possessed and maintained by England; and if the works are made as proposed, and the other arrangements for defence made as proposed, it seems quite impossible to be otherwise than that England, if acting with ordinary energy, should hold the command of the St. Lawrence as far up as Lake St. Louis. But this is not enough:—every possible exertion should be made to obtain and keep the command on the lakes, especially on Lake Ontario. Keeping the command on all the lakes may not be possible, and even maintaining the superiority on Lake Ontario alone will require the adoption of most vigorous measures, and be highly expensive, but is of such necessity that the subject should be immediately considered and prepared for. Carrying up gun-boats from Montreal by the St. Lawrence, and the canals made to avoid the rapids of that river, cannot be trusted to, as they are partly on the right bank, and even portions of those on the left bank are within range of the guns on the right bank, and on islands possessed by America. It is only by the Rideau Canal, therefore, that the water communications could be kept open between

Montreal and Kingston in case of war. It seems essential,
therefore, that it is ascertained that the whole of that line of
water communication is now in a perfect state, or that it is
made so. It is understood here that the Grenville Canal, of
the Ottowa, cannot take vessels of such size as the Rideau can;
if such is the case, its immediate enlargement, which presents
no engineering difficulty whatever, should be forthwith commenced.

25. Naval superiority being an all-important question as
regards the defence of Canada, we must be excused the apparent
presumption of observing here, that, in any future war between
Great Britain and the Federal States of America, it will not
be possible to employ, whether on the coasts of America or on
the lakes of Canada, any other than either iron vessels, or
vessels of wood plated with iron. The Federal States are now
building an iron-clad fleet of gunboats and floating batteries,
and on a consideration of the effects of the horizontal fire of
shell guns, it seems impossible to come to any other conclusion
than that it will be courting disaster to expose in future
unplated vessels to the horizontal fire of shell guns from
plated vessels. The size of large unplated vessels will only
expose them to more certain destruction by ignition, from
their being more easily hit. In the great inlets on the coast,
where the British fleet ought to be so formidable to America,
unclad vessels of large size could not act at all, as the enemy's
small iron-clad vessels, by keeping in shallow water, would,
by the horizontal fire of shells, possess every advantage for
burning and destroying large unclad wooden vessels, without
the latter having any power to get near to them. The expense
and trouble would no doubt be great, but the fact should be
admitted and prepared for, so that, in the event of a war with
the Federal States, the British fleet acting on the coast of
America, and also that acting on the lakes of Canada, may
consist of iron-clad vessels.

26. The number of forts named in this proposed system for
the defence of Canada is 22, and the cost would be 2,200,000*l.*
sterling. The question arises, and would be one of very great

dispute, whether Canada or Britain should be at the expense of those works. It is now a favourite doctrine in England that the Colonies, having got the management of their own affairs, should pay their own expenses. This idea has plausibility, and as regards time of peace may be true. But for each case, and for each colony, a separate consideration is required.

27. If Canada remains a colony of Great Britain, then England adopts Canada as her field of battle with the Federal States, and that in, probably, one of the most expensive wars in which England has been engaged. It is manifestly impossible, therefore, that Canada, with so small a revenue, say a million annually, and unaccustomed to heavy direct taxation, could be called upon to pay more than a very small proportion of the cost of so great a contest. Canada would pay in the devotion and sacrifice of her Militia and Volunteers, and by the appalling ravages and damage done to a country, when made the theatre of military operations ; but the great expenditure of money would without doubt fall on England. It is evident that England must either avoid the contest in Canada altogether, or must carry it on in a manner consistent with her high position. If England entered into a contest for the defence of Canada, she would put forth her power, and, were that power properly directed, would be victorious; but at a vast expense. It is assumed here, that the wisest and most economical course England can pursue in regard to Canada is that of putting that country in a formidable state of defence, by building the twenty-two forts as proposed, which would cost 2,200,000*l.*, and placing in those works, or under their protection, the necessary guns for the supplementary field-works, and the ammunition and other military stores necessary ; so that those measures, together with the necessary preparations for building and collecting a naval force when required, would put the country in such a position that it would at all times be ready to defend itself.

28. We assume that this would be, in all probability, the most economical course to pursue in regard to Canada. This opinion is formed on two considerations—the first is, that, were Canada put into the formidable state of defence proposed, it would pro-

O

bably prevent war altogether; as it would then be seen that the conquest of Canada would be an operation of vast magnitude and difficulty; whereas, leaving that country in an open and unprotected state is an absolute inducement to war, with a view to its conquest. Again: suppose that war actually does take place, England could not suffer defeat in Canada without lowering her prestige and shaking her high position, from which might arise consequences not to be calculated. Every proper effort, therefore, should be made, so far as can be foreseen, to insure success by a carefully prepared systematic plan of defence. It is difficult, generally altogether impossible, to induce statesmen to propose the expenditure of considerable sums of money for purposes to meet future events, the occurrence of which is not absolutely certain. But it is assumed here that this is not the mode to treat military questions. The results of warlike operations are too overwhelming and serious to be left to doubt and chance; all precautions should be taken to insure success, and to prevent disaster, as far as can be foreseen, and so far as can be accomplished within the limits of moderate and reasonable expense.

29. The plan for the defence of Canada, as proposed in these notes, is founded very much on the same principles as those which guided the general plan of works for the defence of England, and which are now, happily, in full progress of execution. Those works are so placed as to occupy the most important strategical points, and their execution is admirable. So long as there is, as at present, in addition to the regular forces, a sufficiently numerous force of Volunteers and Militia to allow of the works in question being fully occupied, and for the occupation of a field of battle to defend London, England cannot have even the slightest apprehension of being seriously attacked. The strength of great intrenched camps consists in this, that they are too strong, when occupied by even troops of inferior discipline, to be taken by assault; and they are too extensive to be successfully invested; and unless completely invested it is next to impossible to take a place by regular attack.

30. Some questions will naturally arise on the perusal of the preceding observations which it may be proper to answer here

by anticipation. The number of men proposed here for the defence of Canada is 130,000 Volunteers and Militia, and 30,000 British troops. It may be asked whether it is meant that 30,000 British troops, or anything approaching to that number, are to be left permanently in Canada. The answer to this question is, that the opinion entertained here is that, were Canada put into such a position from the forts being built as proposed—the Volunteers and Militia organization kept up at a very moderate rate of expense—an ample supply of arms, ammunition, and military stores kept at the places intended as the great intrenched camps—and the proper means taken for the naval defence of the St. Lawrence and the Lakes—the number of British troops left in Canada may be *very small indeed*. It will be asked if Canada would not in this case be liable to attack when the St. Lawrence becomes closed in the beginning of winter. Canada did incur that danger in the winter of 1861-2; but would not be in any danger when prepared, as proposed, for defence; there would then be men enough to occupy the intrenched camps—sufficient of arms and military stores; and in place of the enemy having only open towns to possess himself of, he would be obliged to besiege them, an operation impossible in a Canadian winter; besides which, the communication through Nova Scotia and New Brunswick will be improved. The intended line of railway from Halifax to Quebec by the head of the Bay of Chaleur, if carried out as proposed as a great line of communication, would very much improve, although it would not perfect, the means by which troops and warlike stores could be sent from England to Canada during war, or when war became imminent.

31. It will probably appear extraordinary to those who have considered former plans for the defence of Canada, that the defence of the line of the Richelieu is not mentioned here. It has, in the former systems proposed, been considered essential to defend the line of that river. The view taken here on the contrary is, that by forming Montreal into a great intrenched camp —by having two great *têtes-de-ponts* on the right bank of the St. Lawrence opposite to Montreal—by having two forts and a small intrenched camp at Sorel, to prevent the enemy's communicating

with the St. Lawrence by the Richelieu—by having a fort on the island at the mouth of the Châteauguay river, to prevent the enemy's communication with the St. Lawrence by that river—enough will be done; and that by extending your force to the Richelieu, and attempting to maintain yourself upon the line of that river, you would only weaken your whole position. It might answer to hold posts on the Richelieu when Canada was attacked by the numerically insignificant bodies of men employed in former wars; but should Montreal be attacked by a large force, the posts on the Richelieu will be passed and disregarded; and their fall would be a matter of course, should the great operation against Montreal succeed. Although not stated before, the great importance of a fort on the island at the mouth of the Châteauguay river will now be manifest—by closing the navigation of that river against the enemy's communicating by it with the St. Lawrence; by strengthening the hold and command of Lake St. Louis; and by rendering the investment by an enemy more difficult, from the facilities of sortie which it would add to those from the *têtes-de-ponts* proposed for the right bank.

32. It will be asked—Are then this great preparation, and those great operations for the defence of Canada (if that country is attacked by a very large force), to end in only one of two things,—that is, the mere repulse of the enemy, or his success? In this case Canada may lose, but cannot gain anything. But such is not the view taken here; on the contrary, it is considered that if the great numerical force, as supposed, were to attack Canada and suffer repulse, its defeat ought to be attempted, and such offensive operations entered upon, as would, if successful, lead to a readjustment of the frontier on the termination of the war.[1]

33. Much of the efficiency of the plan proposed here for the defence of Canada depends upon the strength of intrenched camps. The subject has been stated and exemplified in the preceding Notes, but we now propose shortly to bring it more together, and with some addition.

---

[1] Observe that this was written in February, 1862, and that the aspect of affairs may now be different.

Great intrenched camps have the advantage, in defending towns, of keeping the enemy's force at a great distance from them. They are of great strength when occupied by a sufficiently numerous force, although a great proportion consist of troops not fully disciplined; they are too strong to be taken by assault; and in either the case of their surrounding a place on a large circumference, or when they join two points which cannot be turned, it seems next to impossible that they can be worked up to by regular approaches, as the sorties of garrisons so numerous, against such extensive lines of investment as the attacking force must have, ought to be in the highest degree formidable; but in addition to the difficulty of investment, there would be the almost insurmountable one of working up to a place presenting nearly straight lines of defence, and the sorties from which would be the movements of an army acting either against the approaches or any point of the investing line at pleasure, both as to time and place.

The difficulty of an attacking force maintaining a line of investment round a very large place, such as Paris, seems to us to be absolutely insuperable, if the garrison is sufficient, and the people of the country hostile; and this applies in degree to every place so defended.

It seems not to be determined what effect the recent improvements of fire-arms will have upon sieges of places having continuous lines of defence, and that can be fully invested; but the effect will be very great in strengthening all prepared fields of battle, and eminently so in strengthening all intrenched camps. It will be next to impossible to march up directly to attack in front prepared fields of battle,—they must now be attacked in a different manner; and intrenched camps can only be attacked by forces sufficiently numerous completely to invest them, and then to attack them by regular approaches. Thus the great strength of intrenched camps consists in the difficulty of completely investing them, without the attacking force being exposed to destruction by the powerful sorties of the invested force, aimed in repeated attacks at his weakest points. The great principle must be borne in mind, that a place that is not fully invested cannot be taken but under very exceptional circumstances. If the attacking force is in an enemy's country, taking a place without its being fully invested seems all but impossible, as the place would be supplied with food, ammunition, and men, while the attacking force could only be supplied by means of convoys, guarded by a large military force.

The existence of a large force of Volunteers, or Militia, or of both, forms a part of the defensive system proposed in these Notes. The Volunteer system is admirable, and deserves the highest encouragement. But the Volunteer system, being in some degree liable to fluctuation from changes of feeling and accidental causes, should not be calculated upon as a force of unquestionable permanence. The rule ought, therefore, evidently to be, that there ought to be power granted to the executive to call out Militia for the whole number of men wanted, but that never more should be called out than such as would, together with the Volunteers, make up that number. To give an example : suppose that 130,000 men are wanted for the defence of Canada, and that 30,000 Volunteers were organized and ready to serve, then 100,000 Militia should be prepared and obliged, if necessary, to take the field ; and so in every other case to insure the same number of men, whether the Volunteer force be large or small.

34. The writer of these Notes never was in Canada, nor does he consider his having been so necessary for stating principles on which the defence of that country may be conducted. He in the same way stated principles on which the defence of this country should be conducted, without having made any personal examinations of the country. It is, in fact, a fallacy to suppose that, for forming a general system for the defence of a country, and military operations in it, a personal inspection of the country is necessary. For a knowledge of the geography and topography of the country, and of its most important features in a military point of view, the author of these Notes has received much information, by communicating with officers of high rank and great experience, and who know Canada well. He has also been fortunate enough to see valuable military memoirs

and documents that have never been published. Those documents are sufficient to show the opinions which have existed in Canada respecting the defence of that country. Accompanying these memoirs, and otherwise, there is an important body of maps, charts, sketches, and plans, affording highly valuable information. It may be remarked on this subject, that plans of campaign for the greatest military operations known to either ancient or modern history must have been formed before the commanders had seen the countries in which they operated.

The fact seems to be, that, when a general system of defence for a country is laid down on great military principles suited to the general features of the country, its climate, its population, its resources, and its political situation, a commission consisting of naval and military officers, and, say, a civil engineer of the country, is required to ascertain how the general plan can be carried into effect.

THE END.

LONDON PRINTED BY WILLIAM CLOWES AND SONS, STAMFORD STREET, AND CHARING CROSS.

Also published in facsimile in *The Spellmount Library of Military History* and available from all good bookshops. In case of difficulty, please contact Spellmount Publishers (01580 893730).

## HAMILTON'S CAMPAIGN WITH MOORE AND WELLINGTON DURING THE PENINSULAR WAR by Sergeant Anthony Hamilton
*Introduction by James Colquhoun*

Anthony Hamilton served as a Sergeant in the 43rd Regiment of Foot, later the Oxford and Buckinghamshire Light Infantry. He fought at Vimiero and took part in the retreat to Corunna, vividly describing the appalling conditions and the breakdown of the morale of the British Army. He subsequently fought at Talavera, Busaco, the Coa, Sabugal, Fuentes de Oñoro, Salamanca and Vittoria. He also volunteered to take part in the storming parties of the sieges of Ciudad Rodrigo and Badajoz. During these actions, he was wounded three times.

Published privately in New York in 1847, this rare and fascinating account has never before been published in the United Kingdom.

## RANDOM SHOTS FROM A RIFLEMAN by Captain John Kincaid
*Introduction by Ian Fletcher*

Originally published in 1835, this was the author's follow-up to *Adventures in the Rifle Brigade* – and is a collection of highly amusing, entertaining and informative anecdotes set against the background of the Peninsular War and Waterloo campaign.

## RECOLLECTIONS OF THE PENINSULA by Moyle Sherer
*Introduction by Philip Haythornthwaite*

Reissued more than 170 years after its first publication, this is one of the acknowledged classic accounts of the Peninsular War. Moyle Sherer, described by a comrade as 'a gentleman, a scholar, an author and a most zealous soldier', had a keen eye for observation and an ability to describe both the battles – Busaco, Albuera, Arroyo dos Molinos, Vittoria and the Pyrenees – and the emotions he felt at the time with uncommon clarity.

## ROUGH NOTES OF SEVEN CAMPAIGNS: in Portugal, Spain, France and America during the Years 1809–1815 by John Spencer Cooper
*Introduction by Ian Fletcher*

Originally published in 1869, this is one of the most sought-after volumes of Peninsular War reminiscences. A vivid account of the greatest battles and sieges of the war including Talavera, Busaco, Albuera, Ciudad Rodrigo, Badajoz, Vittoria, the Pyrenees, Orthes and Toulouse and the New Orleans campaign of 1815.

ADVENTURES IN THE RIFLE BRIGADE IN THE PENINSULA, FRANCE, AND THE NETHERLANDS FROM 1809–1815 by Captain John Kincaid

*Introduction by Ian Fletcher*

This is probably the most well-known and most popular of the many memoirs written by the men who served under Wellington in the Peninsular and Waterloo campaigns. The author, Captain John Kincaid, served in the 95th Rifles, the most famous of Wellington's regiments, a regiment which 'was first in the field and last out'. Kincaid fought in most of the great campaigns in the Peninsula between 1809 and 1814 and at Waterloo, in 1815, where he served as adjutant to the 1st Battalion of the Regiment.

THE MILITARY ADVENTURES OF CHARLES O'NEIL by Charles O'Neil

*Introduction by Bernard Cornwell*

First published in 1851, these are the memoirs of an Irish soldier who served with Wellington's Army during the Peninsular War and the continental campaigns from 1811 to 1815. Almost unknown in the UK, as the author emigrated to America straight after, it includes his eye-witness accounts of the bloody battle of Barossa, the memorable siege of Badajoz – and a graphic description of the battle of Waterloo where he was badly wounded.

MEMOIRS OF THE LATE MAJOR-GENERAL LE MARCHANT
by Denis Le Marchant

*Introduction by Nicholas Leadbetter    Foreword by Dr David Chandler*

Only 93 copies of the memoirs of the founder of what is now the RMA Sandhurst were published by his son Denis in 1812. His death at Salamanca in 1841 meant that Britain was robbed of its most forward-thinking officer. This facsimile edition is enhanced with additional watercolour pictures by Le Marchant himself.

THE JOURNAL OF AN ARMY SURGEON DURING THE PENINSULAR WAR by Charles Boutflower

*Introduction by Dr Christopher Ticehurst*

A facsimile edition of a rare journal written by an army surgeon who joined the 40th Regiment in Malta in 1801 and subsequently served with it in the West Indies, South America and the Peninsular War. Described by his family 'as a man of great activity and a general favourite with all his acquaintances', he saw action from 1810 to 1813 including Busaco, Ciudad Rodrigo, Badajoz and Salamanca – gaining a well-deserved promotion to Surgeon to the staff of Sir Rowland Hill's Brigade in 1812.

## THE DIARY OF A CAVALRY OFFICER 1809-1815 by Lieut-Col William Tomkinson

*Introduction by the Marquess of Anglesey*

The importance of *The Diary of a Cavalry Officer* for students of the Peninsular War of 1808-14 and of the Waterloo campaign of 1815, as well as its capacity to interest and inform the nonspecialist, is attested to by its scarcity in secondhand bookshops. It is eagerly sought after by both types of reader. There is hardly a serious account of the Peninsular 'running sore' (to use Napoleon's own words), which was a chief reason for his downfall, or of Waterloo, that does not rely in some degree on Tomlinson.

In Spain and Portugal he served with distinction for nearly five gruelling years in the 16th Light Dragoons, later 16th Lancers, one of the best cavalry regiments in the Peninsula.

Some of the important and patently accurate details of many actions in which he took part appear in no other accounts but it is chiefly for the penetrating comments on both esoteric and homely, mainly non-military, situations that the general reader will welcome this reprint.

As a temporary staff officer Tomkinson was at times close to Wellington and his detailed account of the Iron Duke's working day when not actually in the field is unique.

## RECOLLECTIONS OF THE EVENTFUL LIFE OF A SOLDIER by Joseph Donaldson

*Introduction by Ian Fletcher*

When 16 year-old Joseph Donaldson announced to his parents in 1809 that he had 'gone for a soldier', they were understandably horrified, given the bleak and uncertain prospects facing their beloved son, of whom they had such high hopes. Donaldson returned safe and sound at the end of the Napoleonic Wars and the end result of Donaldson's writings was this wonderfully graphic, gripping and often poignant memoir, reproduced here in facsimile for the first time since 1852, along with his two other works, *The War in the Peninsula* and *Scenes and Sketches in Ireland*. In them, Donaldson writes with great skill of his experiences in Portugal, Spain and the south of France, serving with Wellington's army as it fought its way through the Peninsula. His account includes such episodes as Massena's retreat from Portugal, the storming of Ciudad Rodrigo, the storming and sacking of the fortress of Badajoz (a really gripping piece), the battles of Salamanca, Vittoria, the Pyrenees, the invasion of France and the battles of Orthes and Toulouse, all of which Donaldson witnessed as a soldier in the ranks of Sir Thomas Picton's 'Fighting' 3rd Division, the toughest division in Wellington's army.

This is a classic book which ranks amongst the most graphic and enjoyable of the many memoirs of the Peninsular War.

**THE PRIVATE JOURNAL OF JUDGE-ADVOCATE LARPENT:** attached to the Headquarters of Lord Wellington during the Peninsular War, from 1812 to its close by Francis Seymour Larpent
*Introduction by Ian C Robertson*
Originally published in 1853, this is a facsimile of the third edition of one of the five contemporary journals, later published without alteration, which Sir Charles Oman has referred to as being an interesting and not always discreet account of his busy life at Head-Quarters, and among the best for hard facts.

In September 1812, the 36 years old Frances Larpent set sail for Lisbon to take up the exacting position of Judge-Advocate-General with the responsibility of reforming and simplifying the disciplinary machinery of courts-martial throughout Wellington's army in the Peninsula, where no form of professional regulation had yet been instituted.

In almost daily contact with Wellington, Larpent's narrative is of especial interest as being written from the point of view of a non-combatant.

This volume is a "must" for all students of the Peninsular War in general and the Duke of Wellington in particular.

**MILITARY MEMOIRS OF FOUR BROTHERS:** engaged in the service of their country as well as in The New World and Africa, as on the Continent of Europe by The Survivor (Thomas Fernyhough)
*Introduction by Philip Haythornthwaite*
*Military Memoirs of Four Brothers,* first published in 1829 and reprinted for the first time, in the Spellmount Library of Military History, since 1838, is an extremely rare record of the military service of one family during the Napoleonic Wars.

The Fernyhoughs of Lichfield provided four officers to the British naval and military forces, two of whom died on service with the Royal Marines. The letters and journals of two of the brothers provide a fascinating account of some of the more important, and some of the lesser-known campaigns and operations of the period, including the Trafalgar campaign, the expedition to South America, and the Peninsular War, Robert Fernyhough serving in the latter with that most elite and famous corps, the 95th Rifles, later the Rifle Brigade.

Thomas Fernyhough, the brother who compiled the account, was a noted historian and researcher, and produced a book which is not only one of the rarest contemporary memoirs of the Napoleonic Wars, but one which illuminates the services and tribulations of a typical military family at this most crucial period in British history.

For a free catalogue, telephone

Spellmount Publishers on

01580 893730

or write to

The Old Rectory

Staplehurst

Kent TN12 0AZ

United Kingdom

(Facsimile 01580 893731)

(e-mail enquiries@spellmount.com)

(Website www.spellmount.com)